Parker Gillmore

Accessible Field Sports

The Experiences Of A Sportsman in North America

Parker Gillmore

Accessible Field Sports

The Experiences Of A Sportsman in North America

ISBN/EAN: 9783742813923

Manufactured in Europe, USA, Canada, Australia, Japa

Cover: Foto ©Stingray / pixelio.de

Manufactured and distributed by brebook publishing software (www.brebook.com)

Parker Gillmore

Accessible Field Sports

ACCESSIBLE FIELD SPORTS:

The Experiences of a Sportsman in North America.

By "UBIQUE,"
AUTHOR OF "GUN, ROD, AND SADDLE," ETC.

CLOSE QUARTERS.

LONDON: CHAPMAN & HALL, 193, PICCADILLY.
1869.

TO

HENRY LEE, ESQ.,

F.L.S., F.G.S., F.Z.S.,

MEMBER OF COUNCIL ROYAL MICROSCOPICAL SOCIETY, MEMBER OF COUNCIL
RAY SOCIETY, MEMBER OF COUNCIL PALÆONTOGRAPHICAL
SOCIETY, ETC., ETC.,

I DEDICATE THIS BOOK,

FOR A FRIEND, IN THE TRUE ACCEPTATION OF THE WORD,
I HAVE ALWAYS FOUND HIM. '

UBIQUE.

The Waldrons, Croydon,
April 3rd, 1869.

Dear MR. GILLMORE,

Your letter asking my permission to dedicate to me your forthcoming work on "ACCESSIBLE FIELD SPORTS" has gratified me exceedingly, and I accept with pleasure your kind proposition.

When on your return to this country after years of foreign travel, LORD RICHARD GROSVENOR mentioned to me his appreciation of your talents, I did not, of course, foresee that his introduction would lead to our becoming friends. Since then, however, circumstances and kindred tastes have brought us closely together. Intimately associated, as I have the privilege to be, with my dear friend MR. FRANK BUCKLAND in almost all his undertakings, public and private, the love of Natural History which I have felt from my boyhood has been fostered by him, and he has imbued me with much of his enthusiasm respecting pisciculture. I immediately recognised the practical character of your writings on these subjects and on the Field Sports of the many countries you have visited, and if I have in any way aided you in making known the results of the observations you have made during an adventurous life, I congratulate myself and the public on my having been able to do so.

I assure you that the kind and complimentary tribute you now offer me more than repays me for any encouragement I may have been enabled to give you.

With every good wish, believe me to be,

Dear MR. GILLMORE,

Your very sincere friend,

HENRY LEE.

PREFACE.

In producing this Work, I am actuated by the hope that many of our English Sportsmen may be induced to cross the Atlantic; for well I know they will be amply rewarded for their trouble, provided they are of the right stamp, and do not mind roughing it, in search of sport with "Gun, Rod, and Saddle."

The expense is not great for such a trip; the sea voyage, under ordinary circumstances, does not extend over ten days, while the accommodation and *cuisine* on board ship are excellent.

I much prefer the Inman Line of Trans-Atlantic steam ships to all others, and I therefore recommend them, for the reason that the officers are more obliging and willing to afford information than those I have sailed with in other lines.

On arrival in New York, select the Brevoort House, in Fifth Avenue, for your residence; it is conducted in the same manner as an English hotel. You can choose what hours are most convenient and suitable for your meals, while the domestics are always civil. The proprietors of this house can afford reliable information as to the hunting-grounds, the best means of reaching them, and other local details.

Messrs. J. D. Dougall and Son, St. James's Street, London, I can recommend to supply the sportsman intending to go abroad with enduring, hard-hitting, well-finished guns. Their Lock-fast patent for breech-loaders is the strongest known, is extremely simple, and therefore not liable to get out of order; and if such a casualty should by any possibility occur, can be repaired by the least skilful mechanic, a desideratum of no ordinary importance when in a distant foreign land.

For duck-shooting and salmon-fishing wading stockings and waterproof clothing will be found necessary; in fact, without such protection from wet, the strongest constitutions may suffer. Those made by Messrs. Woolgar & Co., Ludgate Hill, I cannot praise too highly. For camping out, the waterproof ground-sheet, and the waterproof boating-bag, both of which are made by the same firm, I can recommend, after long experience, to be superior to all other productions with which I am acquainted.

If rods or fishing tackle, extra guns or ammunition, should be required for the lakes and rivers, or the hunting-field, Messrs. Andrew Clerk & Co. will supply the former, and Messrs. Schyler, Hartley and Graham, the latter; both these firms have their places of business in Maiden Lane, New York, and the utmost reliance and confidence can be placed in their attention, selection, and promptness in attending to your wants.

Follow my advice, and you will not be disappointed.

UBIQUE.

CONTENTS.

CHAP.	PAGE
I.—A NIGHT'S ADVENTURE	1
II.—FIRST DEER IN AMERICA	13
III.—TROUT FISHING ON THE ANDROSCOGAN	22
IV.—WILD-FOWL SHOOTING IN ILLINOIS	32
V.—THE BLACK OR SILVER FOX (*Canis argentatus*)	43
VI.—AMERICAN WOODCOCK (*Microptura Americana*)	52
VII.—BUFFALO HUNTING (*Bison Americanus*)	59
VIII.—ON THE GRAND PRAIRIE	82
IX.—MOOSE DEER (*Cervus Alces*)	96
X.—SHOOTING IN ILLINOIS	115
XI.—BLACK BEAR (*Ursus Americanus*)	125
XII.—FLIGHT SHOOTING ON GRAND PRAIRIE	143
XIII.—SALMON FISHING IN LABRADOR	147
XIV.—PRONG-HORNED ANTELOPE (*Antilocapra Americana*)	218
XV.—PINNATED GROUSE (*Tetrao cupido*)	233

CHAP.	PAGE
XVI.—TROUT FISHING IN MAINE	247
XVII.—INSTRUCTIONS FOR ENGLISH SPORTSMEN	273
XVIII.—MUSK SHEEP OF ARCTIC AMERICA	283
XIX.—SNIPE SHOOTING (*Scolopax Wilsonii*)	292
XX.—HINTS FOR AMERICAN SHOOTING	301
XXI.—SHOOTING IN MISSOURI	310
XXII.—A LONG DEER HUNT	313
XXIII.—THE SPLIT BAMBOO FLY-RODS	330

ACCESSIBLE FIELD SPORTS.

CHAPTER I.

A NIGHT'S ADVENTURE.

THIRTY miles north of Toronto commences a network of lakes that extend over many hundred square miles northward, scattered in every direction through the dense forest that covers that picturesque locality. Game and fish of almost every variety are here to be found, making one of the best retreats for enthusiastic sportsmen that can be found within a similar radius of the Atlantic sea-board of Northern America. True, the prairie chicken, the capricious salmon, and the timid trout are wanting; but this deficiency is well supplied by the number and variety of other species of game well worthy of the attention of both hunter and fisherman. Bear and deer are here numerous, roaming undisturbed in the retreats of their progenitors; while the clear, sparkling waters are well stocked with the voracious muscalonge and the active impetuous black bass. But he who is desirous of visiting this elysium in pursuit of game must be no feather-bed sportsman — no grumbler at imaginary troubles, or shirker of hard work; for, once he leaves the edge of civilisation, no roof-tree will be found to greet the eye after a hard day's tramp, no luxurious downy couch on which to rest his wearied limbs, but, often unprotected, he must submit to the pelting of the pitiless storm. No; he must accept mother earth for his bed, his hunting blanket for his covering, the heavens for his canopy, and—if fortune should favour him with a touch of a north-easter—the leeward of his reversed canoe will give him such shelter as will enable him to keep dry perhaps thirty minutes longer. Knowing what you have to be prepared for, provided you have the constitution and pluck, make a try, and I am certain, on your return, you will be in ecstasies with your trip, recalling with pleasure the hardships you have gone through, and laughing at the little misadventures that chequered (like clouds portending a shower on a sunny day) the tenor of your path. We cannot have all play. Few go through the world without an occasional rub. "Variety is the spice of existence;" and without an odd *contretemps* we should become a very unimaginative, unambitious, namby-pamby lot, unfit for the wear and tear, bustle and excitement, that all must endure before their course is run.

To those determined to accept the conditions, a word on the best sporting gear may not be out of place. First and foremost, a good double-barrel of ten bore, that will throw ball as well as shot; an abundance of ammunition, not forgetting buck-shot; a couple of strong bait-rods, about fourteen or fifteen feet each; several of Buell's patent spoon-baits, reels, &c., &c., with a good assortment of strong untied hooks. Your camping equipments I leave to yourself, or rather to your Indian guide; one thing, however, let me advise — make them as light and few as possible, as many an arduous journey across rugged portages is before you, when you have not only to carry these etceteras, but also your canoe.

Why this rigmarole? some may justly inquire. Now for my reason. Numbers frequently ask me where sport is to be obtained, as they are desirous of an expedition, but know not in what direction to guide their steps. They do not want to travel as far as the vast prairies of the West, and if they did, only small game could be obtained, unless beyond civilisation. Let me, therefore, advise them to make choice of the aforementioned wilds; they are easy of access, and there a large variety of fish and fowl are to be found. Duck in great numbers haunt this locality, as well as snipe and plover, which select this retired northern situation as a breeding place, where they can safely raise their timid, helpless families, without fear of the constant intrusion of the much-dreaded lords of creation.

From Toronto proceed to the village of Orillia, at the head of Lake Simcoe. At this pretty little place you will have no difficulty in procuring one of the Chippewa Indians from the village of Rama, on the other side of the lake, to undertake the duties of Palinurus, for a moderate remuneration. All of these redskins may safely be trusted, and they will be found, not only excellent hunters and trappers, but very obliging, as long as you keep them from the curse of their race, whiskey. Of course, as soon as they leave civilisation, they cannot obtain their dire enemy unless you should give it, or, what is equally culpable, leave it in their way. How I became acquainted with this region was strange and unlooked for. Some years since, having business in Toronto, I was detained longer than I expected, and got both out of funds and out at elbows. Returning from the Post Office much disappointed and disgusted at the dilatoriness of my friends, I turned into a tavern to have a glass of ale, when I chanced to run foul of a former acquaintance who had turned hermit, having built a house on the edge of one of those lovely sheets of water embosomed in the forest several miles further to the north than any of his neighbours. Soon my troubles were all before him, and he, with characteristic hospitality, offered me accommodation for an indefinite period. Next morning we were both *en route* for his solitary home, and never shall I forget the feelings of pleasure and admiration that rose in my bosom when first I beheld this charming retreat, situated on a bluff, washed by crystal water, and backed by the handsomest varieties of forest trees, truly looking to my mind the *beau idéal* of a hunter's home.

After being domesticated some weeks, from the beauty of an afternoon and the coolness of the weather, I was induced to shoulder my gun, and start cross country to Lake St. John, with the hopes of killing some ducks to add to the fare of our already sumptuous table. I had never visited this place before, and as I left the clearing, the last words of H—— were, "Take care you do not get lost." With an amount of confidence, "usually denoting ignorance," I responded that I was too old to be guilty of such a green proceeding. With little trouble I found my destination. Game was abundant and tame, they being overcome with that languor which makes them perfectly indifferent, and which is so frequently the precursor of bad and stormy weather. In a little time my bag was heavy, too much so to be agreeable, and, considering that I had committed havoc enough, I determined to retrace my steps. Another and yet another duck would come in my way, and presented such fascinating shots that I could not resist, so that by the time I had returned to the place where I first struck the water, I was completely loaded. Have any of my readers ever walked two or three miles, with from eight to a dozen mallard ducks in the skirt of his shooting-coat? If so, they undoubtedly have vivid recollections of their weight. If still a tyro, I advise you to make a trial, as a new sensation will be experienced, particularly if the ground is soft and muddy. I had scarcely re-entered the sombre forest, when my spaniel found some ruffed grouse, and treed them a short way off on the left. A brace of these delicate birds would be a most acceptable addition to a future dinner; so, without hesitation, I struck off to the right, to cultivate their more intimate acquaintance. Advancing upon them unwarily, the covey flushed, but flew only a short distance. I thought my chances so remarkably good, that I would make another try, but again the watchfulness of my feathered friends foiled me. With a malediction on my lips, I turned to retrace my steps, but for my life could not

A NIGHT'S ADVENTURE. 7

tell in which direction my route lay. To be lost, pooh! pooh! what nonsense! I was not still a school-boy, and had been too long cut loose from my mother's apron strings. The whole thing appeared too absurd and ridiculous. Off I went, as I thought, straight back to the place I had left; I must cross my own path in a few minutes—only a few steps farther! I am certainly close now! and thus arguing and consoling, I proceeded. By degrees it began to dawn upon me, though much against my inclination, that I was "certain sure out of my reckoning." The more convinced I became of the uncertainty of my position, the more I became excited; at first I walked faster, talked to myself, and tried, though I fear very indifferently, to treat the whole affair as an admirable joke. But soon my countenance became elongated, and a very gloomy expression usurped the place of my previous smile. For change, I shouted, with the hope some one might hear me—a very improbable thing—except, perchance, some solitary aborigine should be out in attendance on his bear or other traps. At last I became fairly desperate, and broke into a headlong run; the pace was too fast to keep up, and fairly blown, wearied, and exhausted, I sat down on the trunk of a fallen tree. The depression I felt will never be forgotten. The terrible loneliness, the perfect solitude and monotony, with the certainty of having to pass the night *al fresco*, made my frame of mind anything but enviable. The mosquitoes, which previously I had scarcely noticed, now put in a claim for attention, for my wretched plight seemed to give them confidence, and they attacked me front, rear, and flanks, and in columns. It was useless to attempt to drive them off; their perseverance would have been most commendable, if engaged in a better cause. Night was rapidly approaching, and the giant shadows had become indistinct in their outline, mingling together in one dark gloom. Distant rumbling of thunder portended a coming storm, reminding me that I had better make all snug, for a dirty night was at hand.

I soon found a prostrate monarch of the forest, under whose side I expected to find comparative shelter; in a short space I had gathered sufficient *débris* and flammable matter to make a fire, determining to sacrifice one of my ducks to the implacable tormentor, hunger. Out of the few matches I had, four missed, or would not light; but two more remained. With what care and anxiety did I try the others! Alas! the head of No. 5 flew off, and but one remained to save me from Erebus, and the incursions of some erratic midnight prowler. With the utmost care I undertook the trying ordeal of squeezing myself into a corner, sheltering my hands with my cap, and sacrificing a portion of the last letter from my lady-love for tinder; success rewarded me, and soon the surroundings were brought out in deep relief by the brilliant glow, reminding me of the deep contrast of light and shadow in one of the much-admired pictures by Rembrandt. The rain was not long delayed, and after a few premonitory drops, came down as if the flood-gates of heaven had been opened, accompanied by the loudest thunder and most dazzling lightning. There is nothing more powerfully impresses man with the omnipotent power of the Creator, or with his own utter insignificance, than being placed alone, unprotected from the warring elements, listening to the dismemberment of limbs from the parent tree-trunks by the fury of the blast, or the scathing power of the electric fluid. All my efforts to keep a good fire were futile—sleep was out of the question—while the incessant attacks of the mosquitoes made me restless and irritable. No sick man or storm-tossed mariner ever more ardently longed for break of day. The night appeared endless, and doubts of whether the sun had not been delayed in his course, or taken his departure to gladden with his rays the inhabitants of other planets, intruded themselves. At last, faint lines of light glimmered in the east, foretelling the departure of darkness, and with greater satisfaction than I ever previously experienced, I rose from my wet and uncomfortable resting-place. To seek my lost route was my first endeavour, and for more than an hour I wandered without success. At last, when almost yielding to despair, I struck the margin of the lake I had been shooting on the evening before; and what a beautiful, enthralling scene lay before me! The placid water only rippled where the wild duck sported, or the voracious fish pursued to the surface their destined prey; while the shadow of each tree that grew near the margin was so distinctly reflected that the minutest limb or twig could be traced with perfect precision.

I stood entranced, and so great was my admiration, that nothing could have induced me to disturb the harmony of the picture by destroying the life, or disturbing the retreat, of the beautiful creatures which formed its prominent features. To the left were several deer and fawns, knee-deep, feeding upon the tender, succulent leaves of the water-lily, the youngsters occasionally chasing one another in sport, and unknowingly practising and developing those muscles which Nature intends to be their protection in the hour of danger; their beautiful, graceful mothers frequently raising their eyes from their morning repast with maternal solicitude for their progenies' safety. What sportsman could witness such a scene without feelings of the greatest pleasure? and, in my opinion, unless hunger could be pleaded, he would be unworthy of the name who could desecrate the hallowedness and peacefulness of the view by wantonly shedding blood. Long I gazed with feelings of rapture, congratulating myself in having at last discovered a hunter's elysium. Uncertainty in reference to my position had vanished, as without trouble, by following the margin of the water, I could find my back track. At last hunger told me it was time to think of home and breakfast. An hour after found me in my bedroom undergoing the luxury of a good wash, preparatory to an ample meal. My friend, who was rejoiced to see me, having dreaded the inconvenience of hunting me up, listened with great pleasure to my glowing, and, perhaps, unintentionally exaggerated description of all I had seen and endured. On one point, however, we were resolved—an immediate visit to the beautiful locality I had so lately left. Before a month had elapsed many visits had been paid, and heavy game bags, or still heavier fish baskets, were the result. Game is still abundant in the region where my night adventure took place, but like every locality, the hunter will have to proceed a little farther beyond the bounds of civilisation; for as certain as the red man vanishes before the progress of the stream of emigration, or the morning mists before the gladdening rays of the rising sun, does game before the dreaded sound of the squatter's axe, or the sharp report of the deadly rifle.

CHAPTER II.

FIRST DEER IN AMERICA.

ALTHOUGH this is but a reminiscence, and one of a day a few years gone by, the feelings, incidents, *et ceteras*, are much the same as every tyro experiences when he sees the first antlered monarch of the woods prostrated at his feet. How many lately have written of their advent in salmon fishing, their novitiate with dog and gun on the boundless heather or golden stubble; but not one has touched on the pleasurable sensations first experienced as you draw the keen edge of your hunting-knife across the graceful, swan-like neck of the deer that has succumbed to your skill as a shot, or your knowledge of the hidden mysteries of venery.

While visiting in Canada West, I chanced to make the acquaintance of a young Highlander ardently devoted to the chase, and who, when he found that I was also a would-be disciple of the chaste Diana, at once proposed, as the season was suitable and business affairs did not interfere, that we should start for the gigantic and then unbroken woods which covered the township of Oro, lying on the edge of that placid sheet of water, so well known for its lovely woodland scenery, Lake Simcoe. After a great deal of bad travelling, both on foot and horseback, over the most villanous roads that ever unfortunate was condemned to progress on, we arrived late at night opposite Snake Island, then inhabited by a remnant of the once numerous and powerful Chippewa Indians. The distance across to this island retreat was too far for our lungs to inform its denizens that two benighted travellers were desirous of joining them, and, as there was no boat, a camp fire and blanket were required to do duty for roof and feather bed. But, alas! our limbs and bones were demoralised from our former life, and absolutely refused to be satisfied, so that both tossed, fumed, and fretted till the sun thought proper to make his reappearance. Nor was that all; a scoundrelly wolf, whose midnight propensity for serenading had taken hold of his thoughts, kept up a most objectionable chant, however pleasing it might have been to his lady-love, till we wished the brute in Jericho, or any other remote district; not only that, but I will not say that fear had not a little to do with my feelings, for I can distinctly remember, as I listened, my blood became exceedingly cold and stagnant, my hands clammy, and my throat parched. Moreover, all the stories I had ever read of the sanguinary propensities of these scourges of the distant settlements, from "Little Red Riding-Hood" to "Robinson Crusoe," recurred vividly to my recollection.

However, quiet came with the sun, and, after a few ineffectual efforts, we succeeded in attracting the attention of a worthy redskin, who, for a trifling remuneration, landed us in the precincts of his island domicile. Our business was soon made known, and a hunting party was organised in an inexpressibly short time. The inner man was still to be satisfied, and, on making our wants known, we were borne off willing captives to the grandest and most capacious log-cabin, no less a worthy than a chief assuming the responsibility of providing us with breakfast. I cannot help here mentioning a little episode which, although it had not the appetising effect of Worcester sauce, chutney, a squeeze of lemon, or other familiar auxiliaries, still had its influence on our then pleading stomachs. Sun-fish were destined for the standing dish, and as the good old squaw had a very small frying-pan and a large stock of the above finny treasures to operate upon, it behoved her to make several cookings; and, to prevent the results of her first efforts getting cold while the second lot were undergoing culinary operations, the aged matron, with a talent that denoted great skill in adapting herself immediately to circumstances, snatched a very battered and greasy straw hat off the head of one of the filthiest youngsters, and made it do duty for dish-cover. Of course, any squeamishness would have been a base return for the anxiety displayed that we should not eat our morning repast cold. An hour afterwards we were all *en route*, three buoyant, graceful birch barks transferring the party, which was now augmented to ten, and three half-fed hounds, to the opposite beach.

Well, all that forenoon to mid-day we tramped, tramped, tramped; the only alteration in the performance being an occasional halt, when an acute observation of some sign would cause comments from all parties, excepting we two pale-faces. First, it would be a broken twig; next, an indentation of the ground; and thirdly, what would not have appeared to the uninitiated a rarity in sheep pastures. Although this was all Greek to us, we determined to look knowing, say nothing, and possibly, like many another under similar circumstances, get credit for being perfect Nimrods. A halt was at length called for, and old Chief John, no small bug, spoke like an oracle. The deer had gone to the big swamp, and if we wanted buck

FIRST DEER IN AMERICA. 17

we must go there. Off again we started, I having come to the determination that the whole thing was a humbug, and that I would slip off the first available opportunity. The desired chance soon offered, and after half an hour's walking I struck the margin of the lake where the canoes had been left. Another I found before me at this rendezvous, which helped much to console me for not being the only deserter. We had not been long dawdling and attempting to kill time, when some pigeons came down to drink; so drawing my buck-shot and replacing it with No. 6, I came to the conclusion, as I could not have venison, I would try and procure some of them. Nor was I unsuccessful, for soon half a dozen long tails (the wild pigeons of America have long tails) swelled the voluminous proportions of my pockets. There is an end to all things, and even pigeons got wary of our proximity, and a second period of inaction followed. However, the scenery was pretty, the foliage brilliant, the temperature pleasant, and a hunter might be far less comfortably situated.

Time was passing rapidly, the sun was fast dipping into the horizon, and consequently our indefatigable friends could not much longer be absent. Thus I thought when Master Redskin jumped suddenly up out of a canoe in which he had been lolling, clapped his ear to the ground, and remained in that ludicrous and ungraceful position for some minutes, exciting greatly my curiosity. On asking him for an explanation, naught but a grunt could I get for an answer, and a non-describable wave of the hand, as if to invoke silence. After manœuvring thus, my nearly exhausted patience received the explanation that one of the hounds was running a deer, and that they were coming this way. Immediately afterwards I was bundled into a canoe, and although I had never previously handled a paddle, was now forced to take one of those implements and attempt a trial; but no use—the obstinate composition of birch bark would only spin round and make most indisputable signs of objection to its freight, which were manifested by the gunwale several times taking in water and almost upsetting, so that my now irate companion almost got out of his wits with rage. At length I attained a slight dexterity, and succeeded, assisted by the skilful steering of the Chippewa, in propelling our frail boat under a cedar that grew on the termination of a promontory. Whatever might have been my doubts before as to my friend's assertion that game was afoot, they were now dissipated; for, true enough, the deep voice of a hound could be distinctly heard resounding through the forest, and coming towards us; every bound the good hound spoke, till the echoes and his voice were blended in one prolonged, deep, musical note. My pulsation increased as the sound approached, my whole nervous system was in a state of extreme tension; even clasping my gun, setting my teeth, only gave me temporary relief, and never from that day to this has my excitement been so intense. "Look! look!" said the Indian, and, following the direction of his hand, I saw a splendid doe breasting the water and heading for the middle of the lake. Like all green hands, my first prompting was to start in pursuit; but my more wily friend put a veto on that proposition, begging me to restrain my impatience till the quarry got well out from land. Long—very long—appeared the next few moments. But it was evident I was not boss*—only a deck hand of very ordinary acquirements. Remonstrance was, therefore, out of the question; so submission, with the best possible grace, was adopted. By this time the doe had got nearly a quarter of a mile out—for few animals swim so fast as deer—when the signal was given to commence the chase. Never did oarsman more energetically pull—never did race-horse more gallantly struggle; every thew, every muscle was brought into play, and what I lacked in skill was made up in *vim*. It, however, took all the dusky gentle-

* American for "master."

man's skill to keep the craft's head straight. For many minutes we did not appear to have gained an inch; the perspiration ran down my face, and even lodged in my eyes; but there was no time for rest, no desire for respite; each succeeding stroke equalled its predecessor in strength. At length, we commenced gaining—a further inducement to renewed exertion — and the paddle was dipped deeper and handled still more swiftly. Inch by inch we crept up, at first slowly, then more rapidly, till but twenty yards severed the victim and destroyer. I was about to drop my paddle and seize my gun, when Master Redskin informed me, "Not time yet!" On we advanced; ten feet at most intervened. Mr. Chippewa gave the desired permission, and as I pitched my gun to the shoulder he veered the canoe a point or two to the left. A sharp report followed, and the water boiled with the ineffectual efforts of the stricken animal. Quickly the birch bark was shot up, and just as the deer was disappearing it was grabbed by the ear, and after several ineffectual efforts lifted on board. Know you, reader, that a dead deer will sink; and although I remembered it not at the time of drawing the trigger, my double-barrel was loaded with No. 6, which at that short range, and pointed at the back of the head, almost instantaneously destroyed vitality; and, however easy it may be to lift a heavy body into a boat, it is a different thing to bring a dead deer into a birch canoe.

On our way to shore we picked up the hound, which was taken on board, and enjoyed himself by licking the blood that trickled from the shot-holes. Feeling fatigued from my severe exertions, I halted for a few moments, and commenced handling our trophy, when the confounded dog flew at me, inflicting a most disagreeable impression of his ivories on the palm of my hand—a habit I believe he had with all, excepting his owner; which peculiarity, doubtless, was much approved of by him, but was far from raising this canine in my estimation.

That night I was the hero of the day—the lion of the hour; an honour to which I was no more entitled than many whose fame has been made through force of circumstances, and whose memory will live when an abundant crop of grass, perhaps thistles, are growing over a hero's last resting-place, and the dwellers upon earth have forgotten that such ever existed.

CHAPTER III.

TROUT FISHING ON THE ANDROSCOGAN.

GOT up at daybreak; morning foggy, with little wind; started to the falls as soon as I had swallowed a cup of coffee. Found the river a little lower than yesterday. Took my stand on the big rock near the tail of the rapid. Tried several flies without success, and ultimately put up two black hackles, one with salmon-coloured body, the other with blue. On the second cast, raised a heavy fish, which I pricked; turned round and took half a dozen throws in another direction, hoping the big one would in the meantime forget his previous rough treatment. Took two little fellows just over half a pound, which I returned to their element. Thought I would give the big one another show, and got fast to him first cast; with all my exertion could not prevent him making the rapid, and taking out nearly all my line; nevertheless, having put the brake on, succeeded in turning him, when he came back to me like a skyrocket, preventing me from recovering the slack. I feared that this run had effected his liberation, but on getting reeled up, was agreeably surprised to find that I still held him. Five minutes more brought him on his side, when Collins neatly handled his landing net, and I had the satisfaction of safely securing a good four-and-a-half pounder. Within an hour and a half I had killed eleven fish, averaging two and a quarter pounds, when suddenly they stopped rising, and all my skill was wasted, for I could not raise a fin. This striking peculiarity in both trout and salmon fishing, which no fisherman can fail to have observed, I am unable to account for. That all the inhabitants of a portion of a stream should desist to feed instantaneously, when a few minutes previously they have been seizing with avidity your flies, is a subject on which I should like to hear the opinion of some competent authority. I remember asking an old hand, whose success in his neighbourhood was a household word, and his response was that a sudden change in the atmosphere caused it. This answer somewhat astonished me, nor could I reconcile myself to the idea that fish which, in the majority of instances, lie some distance beneath the surface of the water, should be cognizant of an alteration which is imperceptible to us. From continued want of success, I changed my position, and removed to a hole some way farther down. After much difficulty from the quantity of brush that grew on the margin of the stream, and carrying a rod among such obstacles, I reached the water. The appearance of the pool much pleased me, but it was difficult to fish, from the timber growing so close to the water, and wading being almost out of the question from the rough and irregular bottom being thickly packed with large boulders. Obliged to make a virtue of necessity, with a short line, and a quick, contracted cast, I commenced operations. My companion informed me that he much doubted if a line had been wet there that season; from the result, I think his statement must have been correct. Scarcely had my flies touched the water, when two beauties, radiant in their handsome golden hues, simultaneously dashed at the deception; one I hooked firm and strong, and soon brought to net: a dozen times did I go through the same performance, only varied by occasionally hooking a brace at the same cast. I feared, with such incessant work, my perfect little rod would get strained, but I was disinclined to give up. Having once filled my large basket, and being in a fair way to repeat the performance, I moved forty yards lower down towards the tail of the stream, where, from the placid appearance of the surface, I had little doubt I could wade. With the assistance of the pole of my landing net, I succeeded in staggering out to a shoal bank of gravel, about ten yards from the brink, and although quite up to the knee, established a firm footing; and each cast rose or hooked a fish. The water appeared to be alive with trout; first one would spring several feet clear of the water with a *vim* and energy positively speaking of determination; another would only barely come to the surface, leaving no other indications of his presence than a miniature whirlpool; while a third would roll over like a grampus, displaying a good view of his golden, strongly-proportioned, handsome side, raising the demon of covetousness in my breast. I have frequently sought for a satisfactory reason for the different degrees of ardour which fish exhibit in taking the fly. I am inclined to believe that much is to be attributed to caprice, and not hunger, for it is very rare to see a heavy fish entirely disengage himself from the water when about to seize the cunningly-devised imitation. Several fine fish had fallen to my prowess, and step by step, with cautious care, I advanced down the river, till I had almost got within casting distance of the bottom of the pool, where the stream was contracted previous to forming another rapid.

In taking my last throw, I was so near the broken

water that my trail-fly was without doubt in it, when, without seeing a fish, I felt a smart pluck at my line. On elevating the top of my rod, I found that a small chub had taken my hook. Reeling up to get rid of the incumbrance, and fetching him to the surface, what was my surprise to see an immense trout dash at the unfortunate captive, and in the twinkling of an eye, I had my reel going at telegraph speed. Here was an adventure, truly, but one out of which I could scarcely expect success. Running out something like fifteen yards, the interloper became stationary, and well I knew he had returned to his sanctum, probably to pouch the bait at pleasure. With but a slight strain upon my rod, I waited on the will of his mightiness, hoping it would not be long ere his royal pleasure would dictate swallowing the booty. Ten minutes, at least, I remained *in statu quo*, when, supposing due courtesy had been extended, I took a slight pull just by way of reminder. Alas! the chub came away, and, being now dead, combined with the rapidity of the water, trailed upon the surface. I was not disappointed —the result was but probable. Commencing to reel up to divest my hook of the mangled *corpus*, I had not more than taken a few feet in when, *mirabile dictu*, the same episode was enacted, and the unfortunate mangled remains of the shiner were borne off, apparently to the same location. Patiently now I determined to rest, hoping against chance, that in sportive mood, while playing with his intended *déjeûner*, his highness would get the point of the insidious hook attached to his royal person. What time elapsed I know not, but my necessary inertness and the disagreeableness of my position induced me to endeavour to bring the drama to a finish. With a gentle strain, I evoked a succession of rapid, quick jerks, admonishing me that I had a gentleman of short temper to deal with. Gradually I continued shortening my line, which, although an unusual proceeding thus early, I succeeded in doing without the least hindrance. Still the dead strain that existed proclaimed that no ordinary contestant was at the other end. In all my previous experience I had never seen a fish come without an effort almost up to my hand, without once making a rush, or giving a chance to judge of his paces. By this time nearly all my line was in, and the trout could not have been over fourteen or fifteen feet from me, but down in deep water, moving slowly in rings of a foot or two in diameter. Whatever some persons might have done, I did not exactly like bivouacking in two feet of rapid stream, with a very precarious footing, and a cloud of mosquitoes singing either a requiem or a lullaby about my unprotected face. My patience exhausted, I inwardly made up my mind, let the results be what they would, that I would force the giant to declare himself. Gradually raising the point of my rod, inch by inch, with a steady motion, to my astonishment I brought him to the surface, giving me a good view of his massive form. The chub was across his mouth, as a spaniel would carry a stick, and devil a hook had touched him! Worse than all, it was apparent, from the constant strain, that my hold of the impromptu bait was nearly at an end. Being humbugged and victimised is at all times disagreeable, and as the laugh was decidedly against me, with a sharp jerk, I disengaged my flies, anathematising the brute which had caused me so much trouble, and sincerely hoping his breakfast would disagree with him. With a flourish of the tail, my tormentor bid me good morning, and I returned to the shore in far from an enviable frame of mind. On my way to the shanty for my morning meal, I scarcely spoke a word, no doubt moralising on the uncertainty of all worldly affairs; but just as I was entering the domicile, with feelings of dire revenge, I told my attendant not to say a single word on the subject, for that I had a plan in my head by which I trusted to wipe off all old scores. With vindictive feeling I munched my food in silence, avenging myself on the finny tribe by the quantity of fish I put under my belt, and only did I begin to feel in a placid frame of mind after I had smoked an inch of my morning cigar. Tobacco—divine tobacco! how much does irascible man owe you! Companion in our solitude, amuser in our idleness, and soother in our troubles, what happy fancies and castles in the air can we build whilst watching thy smoke curling gracefully towards the azure heavens or dingy roof-tree! What henpecked husband has not enjoyed your soothing influence when he has escaped to the safety of his sanctum? The lords of creation owe much to the taste and good sense of Sir Walter Raleigh, the ladies little—undoubtedly the reason that he lives less vividly in our memories than his deserts.

About an hour before sunset I returned to the field of action, armed, however, with a strong bait-rod and a bait-kettle filled with well-selected minnows and chubs. With a determination equal to the undertaking of the most arduous and hazardous enterprise, I mounted a minnow-tackle (don't turn away, gentle fisherman, to hide your blushes; any apologies which are due, I freely tender; remember the aggravation I had suffered), and boldly stalked into the water, a short way above where my tormentor domiciled. In working my way down, I killed several of the smaller gentry, but with these I dealt most cavalierly, they being far beneath my present ambition. At length I reached the very stone on which I stood in the morning, and, with nervous, anxious eye, I made my throw. Slowly the bait swung round, and described an arc of a circle to the charmed spot. A rush, a dash and splash, and away flew my line, the reel discoursing sweetest melody (perhaps not sweetest, for the music of the deep-mouthed pack deserves the superlative degree), and I had my gallant tormentor fast. Every effort that ever was successfully perpetrated by fish was put in play. Down and up the stream he frantically rushed; first to one side, then the other, but all without avail. Ten minutes of these futile efforts told a tale, and the shortened and less vigorous exertions proclaimed an early approach to the finish. Carefully I backed out, step by step, feeling cautiously the inequalities of the ground, till I stood confident on *terra firma.* My attendant waited, with landing net ready, and at a preconcerted signal I gave the word; excitement caused him to act too precipitously, and the splash made instilled fresh vigour into my victim's now exhausted frame. Game to the last, another effort was made for life, and with an impetuous rush he again started for his time-honoured, watery haunts. With a nervous grasp on my rod, I was prepared to give him line; but imagine my astonishment when the slack returned to my hand, minus hooks and leader! The swivel, where they joined, had been worn out, and with a rueful countenance, I stood the picture of desperation. I doubt if the physiognomy of Marius over the ruins of Carthage could have looked more doleful. On my way home, talking the matter over with my *fidus Achates*, we agreed upon the verdict of "served me right," for attempting to immolate so noble a victim in such an ignoble manner, and doubly was I convinced of the time-honoured French adage, " L'homme propose et Dieu dispose."

CHAPTER IV.

WILD-FOWL SHOOTING IN ILLINOIS.

SOMETHING like thirty-five years ago Colonel Hawker wrote a work on duck shooting, which not only lauded this amusement to the skies, but thoroughly and lucidly explained how it could be successfully followed in England. His descriptions were terse and clear, his sketches graphic and true, the whole interspersed with a certain amount of romance, which gained his work many admirers, and this description of shooting many votaries. The result, as might be expected, was that from duck shooting only being followed by those who shot for the market, it became a fashionable sport; and many who previously ignored such amusement, —as much as a genuine foxhunter would running a bagged fox, or a crack shot killing a bird on the ground, —followed the now popular mania, and spoke with as strong superlative expressions in its favour as they formerly would have used in its condemnation. During winter, the coast of England, the fens of Lincolnshire, and the northern portion of France, are visited by numbers of wild fowl. These migratory birds receive rest neither by day nor night as soon as their advent is known. Half-a-dozen mallard is considered an ample recompense for a sleepless night, wet feet, and the cramped interior of a skiff; and so imbued have some become with this passion, that though they may be possessed of wealth and all the requisites of comfort, they persistently follow, night after night, this adventurous and hazardous recreation, confidently believing that there is no other portion of the world where such glorious results can be obtained—a proof of the old adage, "Where ignorance is bliss 'tis folly to be wise."

"Sic venator immemor tenoræ sposæ
Jacet sub frigidi temporo."

It has often struck me that if such enthusiasts could, by electric telegraph or some fairy incantation, be transported from their sea-girt island-home to one of the Western prairies, at the proper season of the year, when the immense migratory flocks of the web-footed gentry are travelling southward from their arctic summer breeding retreats, their senses would be considerably astonished, their former hallucinations would receive a wholesome shock, and their most expanded imaginations be far surpassed. And better than all, these legions of birds are free to every one, the shooter not being in constant peril of writs for poaching, trespassing, and violation of game laws, as every one is, whether rich or poor, who follows the fascinating amusement of shooting in the British Isles. I have little doubt, in alluding to English sportsmen and their ignorance of many of the advantages which America enjoys in this respect, that there are thousands across the Atlantic equally deficient in knowledge of sights which almost daily may be realised, and who, though sportsmen, through lack of experience, miss witnessing scenes that would cause them such pleasure and admiration, that the impression left would never be eradicated in future years.

In confirmation of this, I will state an instance that came under my own observation:—I was shooting on a prairie in Illinois, on the edge of a large slough, accompanied by a gentleman who had been born and bred in a town in the immediate vicinity. As we progressed along the margin of the wet ground a brace of duck flushed; each of us cut down one, the mallard falling to his lot: so greatly was he elated over his success that a person would have imagined that he had never previously killed a similar specimen. This supposition entered my head, and I inquired if he would like to obtain a few more. "A strong desire" was his assent. In consequence I proposed a return to the same spot about sunset, promising numerous shots as a recompense, and, possibly, the pleasure of witnessing thousands of duck arriving on their feeding ground. The evening was eminently suited for the purpose of exhibiting a large show of birds, it being dark, stormy, and threatening, with a rapid decrease in the temperature, strongly indicative of frost or snow. In truth, if I had made a selection, I could scarcely have chosen better-adapted weather. After a tiresome and unprofitable day, we found ourselves back at the requisite station, wet, weary, and fatigued, and not by any means in the best of spirits; still, I did not wish to be the proposer of an adjournment of my promised exhibition, and my friend felt placed upon his mettle, lest he should appear to suffer more from his long tramp than myself, or less capable of enduring the fatigues of the hunting field. How often, if we could read one another's internal feelings, should we find that external appearances are only assumed, and that the companion who ostensibly looks as fresh and capable of travelling for hours, as he was at the time of starting, is suffering from extreme lassitude and disinclination to more exertion, only he is restrained from confessing his weakness by a certain *amour propre* and repugnance to acknowledge himself beaten; at least, I speak from my own experience, and I believe that the majority of men are similarly constituted. If men would but give the same attention, the same pertinacious assiduity to business affairs that are bestowed by the devotee on field sports, it cannot be doubted that their fortune in amassing wealth would be equal to their success in filling game bags.

As the sun dipped in the western horizon, or as near as possible to that time—murky, dark, threatening clouds preventing the luminary from being seen—we entered the wet, marshy margin which bounded our future scene of operations. With much difficulty, and the energetic use of all the *vim* left in us, we progressed slowly and steadily, till we reached the edge of the water, where, ensconsing ourselves in the centre of some of the scattered aquatic-loving brush which vegetated in the vicinity, we awaited the result.

Permit me, kind reader, to deviate from facts, and give a hint to all who love the gun that they may find useful in their future essays against all descriptions of game. I have heard sportsmen, and they gentlemen of experience, condemn Colonel Hawker for impressing upon his pupils the necessity of particular attention to their costume, many thinking he devoted too much time and pains to what appeared to them a very unnecessary desideratum. If any one who peruses these lines should be of that impression, allow me, with all kindly feeling, to take an opposite stand, and assert that there is nothing which will more certainly guarantee your success than paying due attention to wearing clothes that at all times harmonise with the colouring of the ground over which you are about to shoot. I have so many times had convincing proofs of the efficacy of attending to this important point, that I consider it scarcely possible to impress it too strongly upon the minds of all. An instance I will state, out of many others I could tell of, which I think will prove that the grounds I take are strong, and beyond opposition. While sojourning West I made the acquaintance of a good-hearted, kind gentleman and thorough sportsman, whom the uncertainty of worldly affairs had reduced much in pecuniary circumstances; in those days, although I had experience, still, as now, I had much to learn; my friend was, if anything, my superior as a shot, more particularly on wild fowl. On the breaking up of winter in the spring of '65—in fact, the morning after a decided thaw had set in—he arrived at my house at an early hour, and invited me to accompany him on the prairie to kill duck. For some time previously all the water that was stagnant, or had but slight current, had been frozen, and there being in consequence no feeding ground for the broad-bills, they had taken their departure for more hospitable regions. My want of success a few days before caused me to doubt if better results could be obtained on this occasion, but being aware that H—— was better posted on these matters than any man in the vicinity, I shouldered my ten-bore, straddled my Indian pony, and started for what he considered the most appropriate place for doing havoc. On reaching the confines of the prairie, we found that duck had come in, and in myriads. In no direction could we gaze without seeing flights in those strange mathematical figures which they always assume when on the wing. (Query—Are they not proficients in Euclid?) We at once held a council of war, and determined to leave our steeds (having first spread a horse blanket on each to protect them from the bitter blast; for every true votary of Diana is humane, though the virgin goddess herself displayed but little of this virtue to the unfortunate Actæon), and after striking the wet land, to separate, one to take the right side and the other the left. My clothes, through chance, were admirably suited for our work, being composed of that common coloured velveteen which so much resembles withered grass, while H——'s were dark and conspicuous; without doubt, his inattention to colour being caused by the lightness of his pocket and inability to procure more suitable raiment. After four hours' shooting, on comparing results, my proceeds were more than double his, while two wild geese, the most wary of all game, were among my victims, he having failed to get a shot at this noble quarry. I was at a loss to account for this superior fortune, and might have remained long without satisfactory reasons, but my comrade's experience taught him that the difference of colour in our costume was the cause.

But to return to our work. As soon as thoroughly located, we divested ourselves of shot-pouches and powder-horns, hanging them on the bushes that we might the easier use them when required—for once the game commences to arrive every moment is of value. Before we had been stationary many minutes a few stragglers made their appearance, the advance guard, doubtless, of the main body; some old and experienced veterans, I should think, are generally chosen for this duty, as these forerunners are wary in the extreme, and seldom or ever come within gun-shot. However, we were not detained idle, a bunch of mallard passed within range, and a salute welcomed their visit; another and another party rapidly followed in such quick succession that it was impossible to shoot at all. These birds, so far, had only flown past, and as night approached their numbers increased, and we being probably less conspicuous from decreasing light, the open water at our side was chosen for their resting-place. Down they would come on the water, almost imperilling our heads, with the rustling sound of the eagle in the act of swooping upon his prey, while some of their companions, less certain of the security of this halting-place, would sweep round and round our *locale* before they finally selected it. As soon as the birds struck the water they would commence bathing themselves, flapping their bodies with their wings, diving with short plunges, and cutting so many capers that one might imagine them stark, staring mad. The fact, however, is, that all this apparent eccentricity is caused by the necessity the ducks feel of cleaning themselves of the insects about their plumage, as well as the pleasure they experience in finding themselves again in a milder climate, with abundance of food around them, after enduring a hard journey from the stormy North, protracted possibly through a day and night. On arrival, therefore, they wash themselves and arrange their dress before commencing their meal—an example other travellers would do well to imitate. But, as the night advanced, some strangers are mixed with the throng. The dusky duck, the gadwall, the pintail, the blue and green winged teal, shoot past like arrows from a bow, the latter making, with the rapid motion of their wings, a sound not unlike an ungreased wheel or hinge. When the travellers are satisfied with the neighbourhood, they dash down upon the water, causing it to fly in spray for yards around, while the first arrivals welcome the new comers with innumerable quacks. The report of a gun then will scarcely alarm them, and, if they should rise, in a moment they will re-settle, doubtlessly feeling security in their numbers.

Tarry a little longer, friend, it may be too dark to shoot, but a better sight than all is yet before you; be not impatient—don't you hear that strange voice? The geese are coming—ay, and brant, too—can't you hear their noisy chattering? Move not an inch, these fellows have two eyes, equal in excellence to the whole hundred of Argus' placed together. Soon a dark line is seen against the sky advancing directly to us. Honk! honk! honk! comes from its different sections, doubtlessly inquiries from the leader as to the propriety of calling a halt. Keep close—stir not, or think of shooting, till they are over you. You cannot, perhaps, see them fall, but the splash they will make tells the tale. Another and another regiment of these worthies came in till perfect Erebus enclosed us, and further shooting became impossible. Our dogs had been busy gathering the slain, and a noble bag we had. The thermometer continuing to fall, and the appearance of a snow-storm becoming momentarily more marked, we mutually determined to desist, well satisfied with our night's recreation.

It took time and trouble satisfactorily and securely to sling our booty; and if any of our friends could have seen our noble selves and nags strung around with the fruit of our labour, they could not have suppressed a smile. That evening, over a glass of hot whiskey punch, my friend told me that, had he not been a witness to the scene I have attempted to describe, the description would not have been believed.

CHAPTER V.

THE BLACK OR SILVER FOX.

(*Canis argentatus.*)

A SHORT time since, on visiting the Zoological Gardens, Regent's Park, two specimens of this valuable and beautiful animal were pointed out to me, which had lately been presented to the institution by the Hudson's Bay Company. I could not help being much delighted with the fine proportions and magnificent coat, particularly of the larger specimen, as he excelled in size and beauty any representative of this family that I had ever previously seen; although for a long period I had resided in a part of Northern Canada that probably supplies as many of these extremely rare animals as any portion of the American continent, and during the entire length of my residence was constantly associated with trappers and fur traders, *et hoc genus omne*, as well as having a line of traps constantly set that required my daily supervision.

The fabulous value that a prime black-fox skin is worth causes him to be universally sought after; the tawny redskin or the swarthy half-bred hunter when he discovers the haunt of one of these beauties, never ceases day or night to ponder over schemes for his capture; the martin and mink traps are for a time neglected, and every artifice, every trick and ingenuity that ever entered trapper's brain, is at once put into practice. Nor is this fox less wary than his *confrères*, but quite the reverse; and I believe, not without truth, there is no animal more difficult to circumvent. Often of an evening I have listened to the broken English of the snake-eyed aborigines, or the curious *patois* of the Canadian habitant, recapitulating how they all but succeeded on such an occasion, or were rewarded with success upon another. By the bright glow of a log fire, illuminating the unhewn log walls, rough chinking and shingle roof of a frontier cabin, the cold and bitter night being made doubly severe by the howling blast that impetuously rushes with angry noise through the disturbed trees, these narratives of perseverance and hardship form a pleasant way of passing the long wintry night. The cup goes round, the pipe is smoked, and the company, although illiterate and unpolished, possess one great quality—sincerity. If they quaff your health or shake your hand, it is not an empty form, but one which emanates from genuine friendship and unselfish feelings.

There are no distinctive differences between the black and red fox excepting colour, save it be that the fur of the former is much finer; but this can satisfactorily be accounted for by his residence being always in much colder latitudes; in fact, his chief resorts appear to be the intermediate space between the homes of the red and Arctic representatives. Nevertheless, I claim that he is of different species from either of the afore-mentioned. My reason I will state.

The black fox has been known in North America since the first settlement of the country. We learn of one of the Indian chiefs presenting some of the earliest settlers with a skin of this species, as a mark of the high estimation placed on the white man's friendship. Not so with the red fox of the eastern portion of the North American continent. In searching over some old works among the admirable writings on natural history emanating from the pen of Postmaster-General Skinner, now dead many years, we learn that the red fox was introduced into the state of Maryland from England about one hundred years ago. The introducer was no other than the gallant and loyal old soldier, Colonel Guy Carlton, whose name so conspicuously appears associated in all the efforts made by the royal troops to suppress the revolution. This noble old soldier was doubtless a hard-riding and enthusiastic foxhunter. The little grey fox indigenous to the country did not suit his exalted ideas of the noble sport as he had enjoyed it at home, and to remedy the evil he went to the trouble, and doubtless, in those days, great expense, to import the larger, gamer, and more lasting animal. The result was the success he so eminently deserved. The first arrivals were turned down in Maryland, not far from Baltimore. From there they have gradually extended north, south, and west, marking their advent by the gradual annihilation of the grey species. I have had the pleasure for some years of enjoying the friendship of Colonel Skinner, son of the old postmaster-general; from him I learn that he frequently heard his father speak on this subject, and that he has often visited the spot where the first English or red foxes were turned down. From my own personal experience I can state a circumstance corroborative of the fact, that with the *entrée* of the red fox into any section of country the grey species either migrates or perishes. Some years since I lived in a hilly portion of Southern Illinois. On my arrival the little grey foxes were so numerous that with a moderate pack of hounds two or three could be killed daily. I had not been there over a year when, to my surprise, when deer shooting, I jumped up a noble specimen of the red. From that date the grey commenced to diminish, and I am informed by reliable authority that at the present time not a single representative of the smaller breed is now to be found in that district. Audubon, an authority on whom generally the greatest reliance can be placed, regards the black and red fox as simple varieties of the same species. Doubtless he never heard of the red fox being a foreigner, or he would have probably agreed in the decision I have come to—knowing the truth of the red fox's introduction—that the black and red fox are entitled to be regarded as representatives of different species. Nor has the red fox belied his ancestry or deteriorated by his immigration. The keen and persevering foxhunters of Virginia, Kentucky, Tennessee, Carolina, and Georgia, give him the credit of being the most lasting and difficult animal to run down that the forests produce. From the natural differences between England and America, fox-hunting is not only a very dissimilarly-conducted sport in the latter, but one associated with more labour and hardship. The woods are so immense that it generally results in cover-hunting from start to finish; consequently slower hounds require to be used, and every advantage of pug taken. At dawn the Field assemble, so as to catch their quarry with a full stomach, and it is no uncommon thing for the sun to have reached the western horizon and the hunters to be thirty miles from home ere the death whoop is sounded.

But to the black fox. I had often longed to capture one of these beauties during my boyish residence on the American continent. The price that the pelt would bring was a supply of pocket money that I could see no end to; but once, and only once, had I the fortune to almost realise my wish. I had been hunting all day by the margin of a distant lake. Tired and unsuccessful, about the hour of sunset I approached a clearing of a few acres in the forest, where Indian corn had been grown and just gathered into shocks. My companion was a little half-bred terrier, who had endeared himself to me from his sagacity and obedience. As I neared the brush fence which surrounded the opening, with the habitual caution that residents in wild lands learn, I secreted myself behind a stump, and took a careful survey; for deer are fond of corn, so are bears, as well as all the smaller varieties of game. I had not remained thus hidden for many minutes when what I had taken for a charred stump suddenly became animated, and remarkable were the movements that heralded this change. One more glance told me it was a fox of the long-coveted species; but what the mischief was he about? mad surely, and for this reason, no creature in his senses could make such a fool of himself. First he took hold of his tail, and spun round like a kitten, next moment he was turning summersaults, or struggling on his back, kicking his legs in the air, then the tail-trick was reverted to again, and so on. For several minutes I stood transfixed; pug was too far off to shoot at, and any attempt at a stalk was too dangerous to put into practice. But my patience was not severely taxed. With a sudden spring the fox dashed forward; up flew a dozen spruce grouse (*Tetrao Canadensis*), and the black-coated gentleman, with a bird in his mouth, quietly trotted towards cover, giving me a cross shot at forty yards' range—a chance which I was not slow to avail myself of. With the report, pug turned head over heels, but quickly picked himself up, forgetting however his prey, and made for the timber. With rapid steps I gained the bird—small consolation for my disappointment; but my hopes were again revived when my little cur dog took up the scent, and waking the echoes with his insignificant bark, went off as if he intended work. At the best pace I could command I followed, singing every few strides a word of encouragement to my trusty companion. Farther and farther into the woods I advanced, but soon it was so dark that at length, with barked shins and sundry tumbles,

I was obliged to beat a retreat. Several times in the pursuit, when I came to a stand-still, Prince's voice appeared as if he had brought the foe to bay. Now as I halted the same thing occurred, and as the dog did not appear to be much over a hundred yards distant, I determined to make another effort, which resulted in no better success. This led me to believe that my dog came up with the fox, and brought him to bay, but as the latter was the larger, Prince was afraid to lay hold, and on my advancing too close to the belligerents, pug would make off again, to halt when he thought himself out of harm's way.

Next morning I instituted a search, which was unsuccessful; but a week afterwards, when shooting wood grouse in the same vicinity, I accidentally came across the carcass of a dead black fox, partly immersed in a pool of stagnant water, which had utterly destroyed what must have been a most perfect and prime pelt.

Now, although I am convinced that the black or silver fox is not of the same species as the red, I believe he is only a chance variety of the kit or cross fox. Mr. MacDonald, who formerly resided on the upper end of Lake Simcoe, assured me that he has taken the young of this species on several occasions, and that twice he found puppies perfectly black, although the vixen and the brothers and sisters bore the usual coloured coat of the cross species. The cross fox of ordinary colouring, although far from numerous, is not so rare as the black, and the value of their respective skins is very different. Still a prime pelt of the former will often sell for £5, the value generally being determined by the darkness of the colouring. The Indians have an idea that age turns foxes black, and when a dark specimen of the cross fox has fallen into their hands, I have heard them regret that he was not a few years older, so that he might have been black, and consequently more valuable.

Perhaps these views of the origin and species of the black or silver fox may not be new; at the same time, I know that they are essentially different from what has been the belief of the majority of naturalists.

CHAPTER VI.

AMERICAN WOODCOCK.
(Microptura Americana.)

THESE woodcocks are undoubtedly migratory, passing the winter in the genial South and the summer in the North; they are also nocturnal, doing all their travelling at night. From the peculiar formation of the eye, their sight is much better after the sun has declined. Strong light is their detestation, for, judging from their conduct when flushed in the noonday glare, their optics are then of little use, hence the idea that is so frequently current that this bird is stupid. Such is not the case, but quite the reverse, experience having taught me that they are as capable as any other of availing themselves of artifices and hiding-places that are likely to throw out the dog, or shelter them from molestation. This bird, although undoubtedly of the same family, must not be confounded with the European (*Scolopax rusticola*), which is coloured differently in plumage and much larger in size. The woodcock killed in England generally measure about 14½ inches in length, and weigh from 14 to 17 ozs., although one is reported to have been killed at Narborough, of the enormous weight of 27 ozs. I do not here give all the minutiæ of the English bird, for it is not of it that I wish to speak, but only sufficiently to show that there is a marked difference between it and its namesake of the American continent, whose peculiarities I will here, so far as memory serves me, attempt to describe, for the benefit of the young hunter and the sportsman who have the misfortune to reside in a neighbourhood that may seldom be visited by this gamest of birds. Length, from point of bill to end of tail, 11 to 12 inches; across the wings, 9½ inches; weight from 6 to 7 ozs. The females generally exceed these measurements by about 1-10. In shape they much resemble the Wilson snipe (*Scolopax Wilsoni*), only they are more round and compact, the eye larger and more prominent, and wings shorter but fuller. In colour the bill is a yellowish brown; legs and feet of a pinkish flesh colour; claws dark olive or brown; iris, brown; forehead, dirty yellow, with two black bars across the back of the head, and two narrow ones in front on the neck, a finely-pencilled dark line running the whole length of the head, the eye dividing it into two parts, with another similar line underneath, and marking the outline of the lower mandible. Three broad bands of brownish-black pass lengthways and parallel from the shoulder to the tail, divided from one another by a narrow line of bluish grey. . The stomach and breast are of a warm fawn colour, becoming deeper in shade as it approaches the tail and termination of the wings.

This description, I am aware, is far from perfect, or such as the naturalist would demand; still, I think it is sufficiently clear to enable the novice to distinguish what he has got when the first American woodcock falls to his companionable gun. Although this woodcock resembles, in many respects, the snipe, in point of character it is essentially different. For instance, snipe will, in the middle of the day, without any perceptible reason, be seen taking long and erratic flights, ascending so high that the keenest sight fails to trace their course, and again wheeling about in the heavens, as if they were creatures of extraordinary momentary impulses; one instant, with speed, dashing off to the right, and in the next moment returning with equal velocity. Not so with woodcock; they very seldom take flight during the glare of daylight unless disturbed, and then it is short, and only sufficient to avoid, if possible, the intruder a second time disturbing their privacy. When on the wing unalarmed, they rarely elevate themselves above the tops of the neighbouring trees, and are seldom seen before sunset or after sunrise, unless disturbed in their bowery, shady retreats. The descriptions of ground which they prefer are moist bottoms, close-covered woods of second-growth timber, and evergreen shrubs, or dry ridges of maple, oak, and beech, where they turn over the decaying leaves in search of insects. Although, as I have stated, these birds have a strong dislike to taking flight and being exposed to the glaring light of day, yet, in searching for them, you will always find more success attend your pursuit upon those declivities that receive the warm, genial rays of the sun. In spring, when the woodcock are on their migratory journey north from their winter residence, these birds travel singly, but are followed in rapid succession by others, following in each other's wake: consequently, where one day not a single specimen could be seen, the day after they will abound. This has given rise to the erroneous impression that they go in flocks; but during many years' experience I never saw over two or three on the wing at the same time, and then it occurred through the birds having paired, or two or more being flushed from a favourite feeding-place. From what I can learn, I am led to believe that Nova Scotia,

New Brunswick, and Maine are their principal breeding-places, although annually numbers take up their temporary quarters in the middle States of the Union. I have even heard of their nests being found in Georgia, North Carolina, and Alabama; but these are only stragglers, and unimportant, numerically, when you compare them with those that are to be found in their more northern retreats.

The nest of the woodcock is very primitive—composed of grasses and leaves, placed in some secluded spot near the root of a bush, or under the shelter of a fallen log. They commence to lay early in April in the State of New York, and sooner or later as they happen to be further south or north; four eggs are the usual number, although occasionally five may be found. These are about the size of the domestic pigeon's, smooth, of a yellow clay colour, and prettily marked with irregular patches of puce or brown. The young, as soon as hatched, run about like the plover, snipe, and the majority of waders, and at the age of four weeks are able to fly. The mother bird, during the infancy of her progeny, is a most attached and solicitous parent, frequently permitting herself to be captured rather than desert her offspring. What a beautiful example the human family may frequently learn from the apparently insignificant inferior animals!

AMERICAN WOODCOCK.

For shooting woodcock, a sport that I prefer to all other field sports, I prefer the setter to the pointer, for the reason that the former are better protected by their thick coats from the thorns of the briars; again, I have found them less liable to become footsore, with a stronger relish for hunting through damp, and sometimes wet ground; besides, they are more easily taught to retrieve, and are, in my belief, more intelligent. Mr. D——, a gentleman who has frequently shot with me, uses with great success a pair of cocking spaniels, which answer admirably and make an extremely lively and pretty team, but they are rather too quick for a veteran; twenty years ago, I should have enjoyed nothing better than such companions. One thing I would recommend, that for woodcock shooting your dogs have plenty of white in their colour, for unless such is the case, you will frequently lose a point and shot by walking past your dog without seeing him, an annoyance to yourself and a disappointment to your setter.

Before concluding, I would call the attention of all good and true lovers of the dog and gun to a practice that exists in Louisiana, and doubtless elsewhere, of killing woodcock with poles at night in the corn fields, with the assistance of a brilliant torch. Like the noble salmon, the woodcock becomes fascinated or stupefied by the brilliancy of the glare, and falls a ready victim to the club of the midnight prowler. America is now coming to that age that it is absolutely necessary to enact laws,* and insist on their being enforced, for the protection of game and fish. If not, half a century hence, the haunts which now abound with game will be as thoroughly divested of it as the Hudson or Connecticut River is of the princely salmon. Once extermination takes place, it will be too late to do aught but repine.

* This was done last year by the legislatures of nearly all the States.

CHAPTER VII.

BUFFALO HUNTING.

(*Bison Americanus.*)

WHEN studying on the distant and Far-West plains of America the habits of the buffalo (for though this name is erroneous, still it is the appellation by which I knew them, and daily heard them called), or pursuing them to supply our camp with food, I never, in the retrospect of a long and adventurous life, enjoyed such true happiness. The air on these distant plains is the purest I have ever breathed. Frequently on a knoll I have stood, after some unusually hard run, inhaling and enjoying its freshness as the thirsty traveller does a cup of clear cool water drawn from a mountain stream. Each day you perform your allotted work, and no cares are sufficiently weighty to be dwelt upon or procrastinated, to return with redoubled force. Your horses are your companions; hardy and enduring you have proved them to be; and between master and steed a bond of sympathy springs up, the animal being all reliance, the owner determined that the confidence shall not be misplaced. With the true-hearted sportsman, who loves hunting for the pleasure it affords, and the opportunities of studying nature as it emanates from the Creator's hands, carnage when useless is detestable; unnecessarily taxing the endurance of his steed, or paining it with uncalled-for punishment, is a crime he would no more be guilty of than the honest man of despoiling his friend. Again, your gun or rifle, ever a willing servant when properly taken care of, requires no small amount of attention: to no other hands than your own trust it to be cleaned. However high your birth, delicate your nurturing, or boundless your means, to do without the assistance of hirelings, and rely entirely on yourself, is in no way derogatory; on the contrary, it is deserving of commendation, and the benefit that will result in after life from such lessons cannot be too highly estimated. I have known a few months of wild Western life do more good in forming a character than years passed in cities or continental tour; for here the fop forgets his folly, and the timid and nervous becomes self-reliant.

Imagine spread before you an immense plain; all around, in whatever direction you look, the same expanse of level country stretches before you. Such is the prairie. The dear old ocean, as viewed from the deck of a vessel, is the nearest simile I can think of. In both an almost level horizon in each direction is met by the sky. Nothing in either is to be seen to break the stillness, save it be the animal life that have these elements for their home. Although this may be applicable, as a general rule, to prairie scenery, there are portions less monotonous; in places, heavy belts of timber mark the margin of streams that ultimately help to feed some of the giant rivers of the American continent; while as you approach the great vertebra of the country—the Rocky Mountains—hill after hill rises, overtopping each other; again frowned down upon by lofty mountains, beautiful in colouring, soft in their distant outlines, and grand in their irregular and picturesque shape. Moreover, between these hills, almost impassable at first glance, through cañons and gulches you can thread your way, perhaps for many, many miles, when, perchance, a beautiful meadow,* thousands of acres in extent, opens before you, rich and bright in the abundance of its grasses, while the slopes that gird these retired retreats are covered with the densest and loveliest of indigenous trees. Such spots as these are a naturalist's elysium, for game of every variety select them for retreats. The buffalo cow comes to them frequently to calve; the worn-out,

* In America termed Park.

fierce-looking bull, over whose head so many years have passed that he no longer has strength to keep pace with the migratory herd, and struggle in its dense phalanx for female favour or choice croppings of pasture, retires to them to spend in abundance the winter of life; while the graceful deer, the timid hare, and the sagacious beaver, here pass their lives in peaceful, happy contentment, except some adventurous white man or snake-visioned redskin should pay it a visit, destroying, as man ever does, the serenity that reigned around previous to his advent.

But come, the morning has broken clear and invigorating, breakfast has already been discussed, and the horses have got a rough rub over. The neighbourhood is well suited for a gallop, for from the slight shower of the previous evening the soil is springy, and fewer of the indefatigable little burrowers—the prairie dogs—have undermined the vicinity. Meat is wanted, and as we start our minds are made up that, unless successful, the sun must dip the western horizon ere we return. Attending our own nags, and giving an extra pull upon the girths ere getting into the saddle, at a sober, steady pace we start. An old practised buffalo runner (for so the Western man terms his favourite and experienced horse) will quietly settle to his master's will, for from experience well he knows that probably a hard day's work is before him, and all his strength will be required; while the youngster or griffin at this work frets and prances, almost pulling his rider from the pigskin. Forbear, rider; curb your annoyance; give and take a pull upon your snaffle; soon the youngster will settle down, and this day's work will probably teach him a lesson that will act advantageously on his future conduct.

Discussing subjects suitable for such occasions, miles are passed; so far, with the exception of numerous bleached bones, or an occasional deer or antelope track, no indication of game has been seen. From a knoll a survey is made, a fresh hole or two is taken up in the girths, and the scarcity of game commented upon. To the Indian, of course, the blame is laid; war parties or moving villages of redskins are always saddled with being the cause of every disappointment and annoyance in wild life. But look there! What is that? A distant cloud of dust. Buffalo for a thousand, and advancing towards where the hunters are stationed. How is the wind? is inquired. One wets his fingers with his saliva, and holds it up. In a few moments the position is declared untenable, and both vaulting on their horses, hurry off to get more to leeward, availing themselves of a swell in the prairie to keep *perdu*. Having marked well the direction in which the herd is advancing, keeping as much out of sight as possible, scarcely speaking a word, and then not louder than a whisper, the distance between the hunters and game is rapidly diminished. From the nature of the ground, no longer can they remain hid, so, taking their horses well in hand, forward they dash, and, in a few strides, what a sight is before them! Cows, bulls, and calves, all intermingled, forming a straggling drove of thousands, heading in the same direction, and feeding as they progress. Occasionally this harmony of action is disturbed. Two ragged, clumsy-looking, veteran bulls approach each other—perhaps they have been former rivals for some dusky-hided beauty's favours. With a deep bellow one throws down the gauntlet, which the other is not loth to take up; and, with fire flashing from their partially-hid eyes, each rushes at the other; but the herd have become alarmed—a foe equally dreaded by both bulls is at hand; their rencontre will brook delay to be settled at a future date; and, with a startled stare and toss of the head, both turn and rush off after the herd, which is already making a most hurried stampede. However, when the hunters are old hands, the bulls might have saved themselves the trouble: while young cow-beef is to be obtained, none but the veriest novice would think of wasting ammunition on their rough and rugged old carcasses. No time is now to be lost. These animals, unwieldy as they appear, for a mile or so are wonderfully swift, and if they should gain rough ground will beat an indifferent horse. Sitting well down in their saddles, nags in hand, and gun resting across the tree, at a grass-country pace, both push for the sleekest and squarest looking cows they can mark. The pace commences to tell, the distance that separates sportsman from quarry is rapidly diminishing, a few strides more and one ranges alongside; the gun, which has been just taken in the right hand, has its barrel depressed; low down, and eight or ten inches behind the shoulder, is the spot, if shooting forward.

A puff of smoke is seen, followed by a report. The *coup de grâce* has been administered by a master-hand, for the huge animal loses the power of its fore-feet, comes down on its shoulders and head, and nought of life is left but a few spasmodic struggles. But where are the hunters? Look well among the retreating herd, and you may occasionally catch a glimpse of their hunting-shirts. A few moments more, and another shot is fired. This time not so successfully. Again the gun speaks; still the quarry retains her legs, but blood is already pouring from her nose, an indication that surely tells of speedy demise, so stop, let the poor creature die in peace—aggravate not her last moments.

The scene which I have tried to describe took place about ten miles on the south side of the Yellow Stone. An old and tried friend from Germany was my companion, and on this occasion we each killed two cows. Double the number, or even more, could have been shot without trouble; but the requisite amount of beef had been obtained, and I was jealous of husbanding the strength of my horse, for then, as now, but little reliance could be placed on the professed peaceful intention of the Indians.

The range of the buffalo was at one period much more extensive than at present. The same reasons that have decreased, and in some instances almost annihilated, other genera, can be safely urged as the cause of this—the cultivation of wild lands and the unprecedented increase of inhabitants on the American continent. On the eastern limit of the Grand Prairie, in Indiana, I have frequently found bones of the buffalo, telling too plainly that this had once been his home. At the present day, at least twelve hundred miles farther westward must be traversed before the sportsman can hope for a chance to use his rifle on this game; and year after year farther distances will require to be journeyed to accomplish this purpose. Their southern limits are Northern Texas and New Mexico, while the intermediate expanse up to 65 degrees of north latitude, according to the season, contains them in more or less abundance. Of late years their range north has been increased between 3 and 4 degrees, so that Indians who formerly had to come two hundred or more miles, if desirous of obtaining a supply of beef for winter use, have the animals now on their home hunting-grounds. I am disposed to believe that this is caused from their finding these northern regions less disturbed—for this is far north of where the constant tide of emigrants crosses the plains—and that the poor, persecuted creatures prefer suffering from the cold of these inhospitable localities to facing the dangers that always are connected with a rencontre with the paleface. Although the buffalo can endure a great amount of cold, and can find food even after a thick covering of snow covers the earth, yet he is not provided like the musk sheep for an Arctic winter, and from his greater bulk requires so much food, that a protracted sojourn in the northern barrens must ultimately have the result of reducing his strength, and therefore his fitness to cope with the severity of the climate. Again, he has other enemies as well as man. The wolves seldom leave him alone. Day and night they bestow upon him the most devoted attention. However, as long as he is in good health he has little to fear from the marauder; but the moment that accident, sickness, or loss of strength from starvation occurs, the buffalo's unhappy position is known, and half-a-dozen of these robbers will remain by him night and day, watching for an opportunity to complete the wreck; and should not this occur as soon as desirable, sometimes they will make a simultaneous assault, one pretending to fly at the victim's head, while another attacks in the rear, endeavouring to cut the hamstring, in which they invariably succeed unless the presence of man should disturb them.

On one occasion, while hunting, I obtained an excellent opportunity of witnessing one of these encounters. At the distance of half a mile I perceived an old bull going through a variety of eccentric movements, at the moment perfectly incomprehensible. To know what might be the cause, as well as perhaps to learn something new regarding this species, I left my horse and made a most careful stalk without once exposing myself, retaining the advantage of wind till within a hundred yards of the old gentleman. The ground in the vicinity was much broken, and before attempting to obtain a survey of the situation, I ensconced myself behind a boulder. I had been eminently successful, the first glance told me. There was the bull pretending to feed, while four prairie wolves were lying around him on the sparsely covered soil, tongues out, and evidently short of breath from some excessive exertion. None of the *dramatis personæ* had seen me, and I chuckled in my shoes as I grasped more firmly my double-barrel, knowing how soon I could turn the tide of battle. By the way, the prairie wolf has always been a favourite of mine, as well as his half-brother, the coyotte. Their bark has often recalled pleasant memories, and their services have several times recovered a wounded deer. In a few minutes the apparent ringleader of the quartette got up and shook himself. This was the signal for the others to get upon their pins. Prairie wolf number one walked quietly towards the bull, occasionally stopping (I believe after the manner of dogs to pluck grass); then, with a sudden spring, made a feint at the persecuted buffalo's head. The buffalo in his turn lowered his *os frontis*, and rushed a few steps to meet him; but this was unnecessary. Now the rest of the fraternity rushed up. Another took the post of teaser, while our friend number one dropped in the rear; and when a second feint at the head was made by his comrade, number one, watching his chance, left a deep scar over the bull's hock. Again and again this game was played, the same wolf always retaining his rear position. Is not the instinct of animals most similar to the reason of man? Here each wolf had his allotted work—doubtless that which was best suited for his capacity. The rear assault was the most dangerous; for a kick well directed would unquestionably have caused instant death to the adventurous assailant; but the most experienced and expert had selected the post of danger and honour. The flashing eyes and foaming mouth of the bull told plainly the result; so I stepped from my concealment. However, all were so occupied that until I awakened the echoes with a loud "war-whoop" I was unseen; but man's voice always has its effect in cases of this kind. The vermin, with startled stare, plainly asking what the deuce right I had to interfere, sulkily trotted off as I advanced; while the persecuted, in return for my kindness, lowered his head, and pushed rapidly for me, compelling me to seek safety in flight. Such conduct in the buffalo was scarcely commendable, and very unusual. I accounted for it by the harassing his temper had suffered, as well as his feeling how inadequate his strength was for escape by flight.

Poor old creature, his days were numbered, for as soon as my back was turned, and a safe distance intervened between us, the wolves returned, and as I rode homewards, occasionally turning and halting to watch the gradually more indistinct belligerents, the victim was still employed in battling for life. After all, was he not paying the debt of nature, and dying as his ancestors for generations had died before him? Man yields his spirit to the source from whence it emanates, on a luxurious couch or humble straw bed, after frequently suffering from protracted and painful illness. The veteran buffalo, effete from age, after a long and happy life, when unable to keep with his companions, dies in a gallant and short struggle, overpowered by his too numerous enemies, a death worthy of a hero.

The cow produces her calf in spring, although I have, on several occasions, met with a mother as late as the end of July with a youngster by her side, not over a couple of weeks old. The attachment shown by the parent for her offspring, and the solicitude she evinces for its safety, impart a touching lesson, which even the human family would do well to follow. I remember on one occasion I had been setting traps in a small stream that had abundant signs that beaver were numerous in the vicinity. I had waded up this watercourse for upwards of a mile, all the time being hid from view of animals on the prairie by the bluffness of the banks. Having performed my task, I left the stream and ascended to the level of the country. The first glance I took disclosed a beautiful and interesting picture, for a young cow, with her calf almost between her legs, stood determinedly facing several wolves. The baby was evidently sick, and the instinct of the party of prowlers told them so, and so far the attached mother had kept them off. My sympathies, of course, were not with the aggressors, and, the better to prove it, I picked out the apparent ringleaders, doubling one up with the first barrel, and accelerating the retreat of another with the second; for although he did not drop, an ominous "thud" gave him a hint that the neighbourhood was dangerous, and that he had better leave it while he had the power.

In September the rutting season commences, and furious encounters between the bulls take place; their actions on these occasions remind the spectators very much of domestic cattle. The combatants at first stand apart, eyeing each other with flashing orbs, while they paw up the soil with their feet, throwing it frequently higher than their withers; their short tails lash their sides, and occasionally they bellow in a low guttural voice, working themselves into a fury; their horns are dug into the soil, and the vegetation scattered to the winds. At length they rush at each other; the shock sometimes brings one or both to their knees; this is repeated again and again: for over thirty minutes frequently, when well matched, the struggle will be protracted. At length the weaker commences to give way, first slowly, always keeping his head to the foe, till with sudden energy he wheels and leaves the victor triumphant. All this time the cow has stood by, an inert spectator, waiting for the hero of the hour to claim her love. These battles seldom or never terminate fatally. They occur at the period when the coat is in the greatest perfection, and the almost impenetrable mane which densely covers the brows and forequarters is unquestionably of the greatest service as a protection. It is my belief that when the sexes thus mate, the male remains faithful to his spouse, for up to within a month of the cow's confinement both keep together. Early in autumn the bulls are in good condition, but after the rutting season they gradually lose flesh, and by midwinter have become so poor that they are scarcely fit for food. The cow, on the other hand, keeps fat, and even in spring fat may be found along the vertebræ and lower portion of the carcass an inch thick.

With the advent of the first mild weather, even before the snow has disappeared, they commence to shed their rough coat, first from between the fore legs, then the prominent parts of the body, and later from the fore limbs and hump. This long hair—or, as it is frequently called, wool—comes off in patches, trees and rocks being used to rub against; the result is, that by March a more ragged, tattered, weather-beaten creature can scarcely be imagined. The horns of both bull and cow are about the same length; those of the former are thick, blunt, and clumsy, while the latter are sharp, slim, and trim-looking. Both sexes much resemble each other; at the same time the figure of the female is more delicately formed, and not within a couple of hands as high at the shoulder, nor is she clothed with such a quantity of the rough, coarse covering over the fore quarters.

When a herd of buffalo are alarmed by the approach of the hunter, the cows in a few seconds head the retreating herd, closely followed by the yearlings and calves, while the lumbering old bulls, from incapacity, drop in rear. When not disturbed, in lying down or rising they exactly resemble others of the *Bos* family; but if they be come upon unawares by an object of fear, the velocity with which they gain their legs and break into a gallop is truly surprising. They are excellent swimmers, and have no hesitation in entering water; nevertheless, annually, great numbers are drowned; but this generally occurs in spring, when the broken ice is clearing out of the streams. Throughout the Western country there are numerous quagmires, and frequently unfortunates get imbedded; it appears, in such cases, that without exerting themselves they submit to their fate. I have formed this conclusion from having unseen perceived a bull get into such a scrape. I watched him; inch by inch he kept sinking, still I felt convinced that a protracted, energetic struggle would take him across to *terra firma*, yet no such effort did he make. Thoroughly believing that his earthly course was run, I advanced to have a closer survey of the finale. The unfortunate did not see me till within a few yards; but when he did, his habitual fear of man predominated over all other feelings; again and again he plunged forward; dread of my proximity had given him strength and endurance, for after a few minutes his feet got on soundings, from which the margin was gained, and the brute was once more free. I think this apathy to death in certain forms is common to the majority of animals.

The dangers attending the chase of this noble game are very much overrated. True, a horse may put his foot in the burrow of a wolf, swift fox, or prairie dog, and send his rider sky-rocketing on his head. The result might be a broken neck, or if such a fall took place when in the centre of a large herd, trampling to death might be possible; but I am convinced from long personal experience that, so long as the game can keep going, they will seldom or never turn on pursuing man. At the same time, if you fire at a buffalo as you ride past him, without much changing the direction they are pursuing, he or she may slightly deviate towards the pursuer. However, your bridle hand should invariably sheer your steed from the quarry, not only to avoid this deviation, but to clear the animal if it drop to shot. The majority of horses accustomed to this work do so of their own accord. At the same time I should particularly caution the tyro that on himself and his own nerve he should invariably rely, not on that of his dumb companion. To be a good horseman of course is particularly desirable, and the person who can ride bare-back will often come in for a run when a saddle may not be at hand. Many of us of course can ride in this primitive manner; but there are very few Americans or Europeans who can compare for a moment in this respect with the Indians—they appear so perfectly at home on their horses' backs: anywhere and everywhere they place themselves, and but seldom get a fall. Many a fat cow I have killed without saddle. However, the paces of horses are so very different, that some I used for running buffalo I preferred riding with blanket and a surcingle; on others I did not feel sufficiently at home without the saddle. For some months I had an under-sized chestnut, very little over fourteen hands. My associates called her a mustang. In some points she much resembled one; but there was a well-bred look about her small head, narrow muzzle, broad forehead, and lean neck, that told of aristocratic lineage. Moreover, she was very fast and high couraged, as well as easy in her paces. Her back, while in my possession, was seldom crossed by a saddle, although she was the favourite mount, and as such was more frequently used. I purchased her for a trifle from a fellow with " villain " plainly written on his countenance, and, as might have been expected, she was recognised and claimed. To part with her was a great trial; but I had the satisfaction of learning that my surmises of her parentage were correct, her sire being thoroughbred, and her dam a mustang.

When buffalo are so severely wounded as to feel incapacitated for further flight, they will then sometimes turn to bay. When this takes place, unless the animal be an old bull, you may safely conclude the wound mortal, and that but an hour or two will elapse before death comes to their relief; but if you be desirous to terminate the final sufferings, when dismounted, be very cautious how you approach to deliver the *coup*, for with velocity almost marvellous they will dash at their tormentor, gathering all their energy for the occasion. A bull I had disabled stood at bay, and, judging from appearances, was within a few moments of dropping; blood flowed profusely from his nose, and already he had commenced to straddle his legs to support his towering carcass. Carelessly I approached. The manner of the rider was infectious on the steed. When twenty yards distant from me down went his head, and at me he sprang. The activity of the horse alone saved me, and the shave was so close as to be far from pleasant. It was a cleverly executed charge, and a fitting finale to life. The impetus of his motion he was unable to control. The strength of the body was unequal to his courage of heart, for, ere he could halt, over he rolled to rise no more. In hunting, as in civilised life, it is dangerous to trust in appearances,—we know how often they are deceptive.

The visitor to the plains desirous of hunting buffalo, and doing so comfortably and under the most advantageous circumstances, should always take his saddlery with him. A hunting-saddle from Peat or Wilkinson and Kidd, made of the best pigskin, would be my choice, remembering always to be provided with spare girths. The high-peaked saddle, generally used in the West, has advantages for frontier use; but for a firm seat, hard and rough riding, give me our English production. A double-reined snaffle I would take in preference to all bridles. At the same time much depends on how a horse is broken. If the nag in his youth had his jaws dislocated with a barbarous Mexican bit, a snaffle will have no more power of control over his actions than officers over a panic-stricken regiment. I once possessed such a beast. The rider with a snaffle might as well have pulled at a stalwart oak as at this creature's mouth. He was a light-necked, star-gazing, hot-tempered beast. The number of scrapes he got me in was so numerous that to this day I wonder he did not break my neck. At Cambridge, in England, I hired from a livery-stable a counterpart of this animal for a day with the neighbouring fox-hounds. There was not a fence I ran him at that Bucephalus did not appear to see till he was almost on it. Marvellous to say, he retained a good place in the hunt; and, still more wonderful, got home without himself or his rider having any broken bones. General Williams—a steeple-chase horse who long contested with Zigzag for the honours at the various race-courses in the vicinity of New York—was just such another. I crossed him once with the intention of a preliminary gallop before riding him in a flag race. However, I found the preliminary more than sufficient. As to lifting him at a jump, or saving him as he lighted, why you might as well have attempted to fly as do either.

Of the arms most suitable for buffalo shooting from horseback, I believe the old-fashioned, large-bore duelling pistol the best. They are easily loaded while on the gallop, for the butt can be placed between your thigh and the flap of the saddle, and thus held. However, to save an occasional use of ramrods (and if your bullet goes home tight, this cannot be avoided), and for shooting with a depressed muzzle, they are absolutely necessary. The breech-loader pistol, on the central fire principle, must be excellent. For my part I used a double-barrelled shot-gun, with the barrels reduced to twenty-two inches in length. The stock, however, was always inconvenient, particularly when loading while the horse was going at speed. Small-bored arms are to be avoided. The trappers and professional hunters use them; but the reason is that they require much less ammunition than those of larger calibre; and at the same time, in killing fur-bearing animals, the pelt does not become so much torn. A small bullet, when properly placed, will do its work instantaneously; but deviation of a few inches is so frequent in this, which may be called snap shooting, that the more severe shock and larger wound of the big projectile are eminently more effective.

BUFFALO HUNTING.

If the reader be a dweller in any part of the civilised earth, and a sportsman of means, I sincerely advise him to essay a trip to the plains for buffalo shooting; but if he be a resident of old England, and a follower of Nimrod, then his remissness in not proving America's sporting resources is unpardonable. The duke, marquis, or baron, may have his grand preserves well stocked with game, and well protected; but the American has the indigenous buffalo roaming in a state of nature over his original haunts, a description of game so noble that in no portion of the world can his superior be found.

CHAPTER VIII.

ON THE GRAND PRAIRIE.

The events which I am about to narrate were not written on the ground, for the simple reasons that it was often difficult to obtain a comfortable, quiet corner, where a man could collect his thoughts, and, perhaps better still, that generally I was so fatigued, after a hard day's work, I was disinclined to deprive myself of the pleasure of discussing with my companions the adventures and results, mishaps, bad and good shots, or anything else, which so happily, and not the least agreeably, form a portion of a sporting tour. On this occasion we had the fortune to discover a venerable countryman, who relied on his gun for a living, and as his business did not appear a paying one, our party agreed to take him into our service, giving him distinctly to understand that one of his duties would be gun-washing. Well, he proved quite up to the mark, and took that disagreeable business off our hands most satisfactorily, giving us more time to enjoy the social weed, and no less companionable glass, spinning yarns of deeds performed, shots made at miraculous distances, and anecdotes of dogs and previous shooting companions. During the early portion of our excursion the weather was excellent, but the latter two days rain never ceased, causing us to take home a much smaller quantity of game than we had anticipated.

On the first day we breakfasted at seven a.m., and on rising from the table found the team waiting, according to orders. But few minutes were necessary to stow in our traps, and get under way. Near the confines of the village (Kent, Indiana) we found birds, but our driver (who was a regular Tom Draw) would not allow us to alight, insisting that we must go first to our intended day's sporting ground. About forty minutes took us there, our charioteer beguiling the time with innumerable anecdotes and songs, never being silent for a moment. One ditty he was particularly attached to, which I can scarcely forget, he having sung it at least a dozen times:—

> "My health and wealth declining,
> The doctor was called in;
> He spoke to me so serious—
> He spoke to me so plain—
> 'You've racked your constitution
> By getting drunk again.'"

However, the warning that the medical attendant appears to have given him seemed to be thrown away, for he drank more spirits, with more gusto, and that without showing the effect, than any representative of the genus I ever previously met.

Arriving on the ground, we determined to hunt Beau and Belle, and keep Jock and Fan for the afternoon. Leaving our waggon by the side of an Osage orange hedge, separating the prairie from a large cornfield, and having inserted cartridges in each barrel, we commenced work. The ground we intended first beating was rolling prairie, with a sufficiency of grass on it to make the walking good, and the cover tolerable. My companions and self stretched into line and started with the wind in our faces. Before progressing a hundred yards Belle set dead as a statue, and Beau immediately backed. Steadily we walked up to the dogs, expecting immediately to commence fire upon a pack of pinnated grouse; but what was our disappointment to find that the dogs were standing to a covey of partridge (*Perdrix Virginiensis*), scarcely half grown: so we let the young ones go without molestation, and continued our range. Our previous forbearance was soon rewarded, for twenty yards farther our setters again drew on game, Beau now having the lead. Up we went, and although alongside the dogs, nothing showed. By coaxing they advanced farther, and lay down. There was no mistake now; this indication I seldom knew to fail. Short was the period of suspense, for up the grouse commenced rising, not all together, but by twos and threes. Each gun killed two birds at the first fire, and not being delayed in loading, our dogs were soon ordered to retrieve. Belle had not gone five paces to perform this duty when she again stood, and bang, bang, from all our guns followed; in five minutes we had fifteen birds on the ground, and more flushing every moment. What luck we were in! We had evidently got out of bed on the right side this morning, and were in for a big day's work. In retrieving the birds two more fell to our aim, making seventeen out of the covey, a pretty good account; and, better still, those that had not been shot at, did not continue their flight more than a hundred and fifty yards, when they lit on the brow of a sunny bank. Having bagged our game, and handed them to Hank (for that was our charioteer's name), we progressed after the balance, and soon were at work again; the dogs struck them off at once, and save that two escaped, who were out of bounds, and took a lengthened journey out prairiewards, we bagged all.

Hank now returned, and gave us the satisfactory

information that there were plenty more, but at the same time adding, "Look you here, jist leave some to breed." We found that our fat friend was correct, for before ten minutes we were again enfilading a second covey. I must tell you how splendidly Beau found this pack. When ranging two hundred yards off, at his usual swinging gallop, he stopped, and sticking his old knowing head perpendicularly in the air, commenced walking straight forward, with a delicate, careful step, well suited for progression over eggs. As I had seen him do so previously, I knew what was coming, and called my friends' attention, so that they might gradually close up towards the faithful canine. Belle soon saw what Beau was up to, and followed him with equally cautious, gingery steps. H., who was off on my right, flushed a bird, which he cleverly cut down with his first barrel, making a very pretty cross shot. But where were the beauties? Both down in the grass waiting for us to come, nor could they be persuaded to leave the game they were on to find the victim first killed. After looking for a few moments, we gave it up, I marking the place as near as I knew by dropping my white pocket-handkerchief, intending to return as soon as I had learned what the dogs had found. As we advanced, Beau and Belle rose, and continued drawing for near a hundred paces more, when they stood. O that some artist had been there to sketch them on the spot! Nothing would I grudge for the picture. The attitude of setter or pointer, when standing, is to me the personification of grace and beauty. Well, the old story: the birds were put up, so packed that we all had difficulty in singling birds; five more fell to our lot; the balance, after going about sixty rods, dropped, scattered among a thick growth of ironweed. The dogs must, on this occasion, have winded their game at least two hundred yards off, so strong is the effluvium emitted by this game and noble bird. In reading, the other day, in a sporting periodical, I noticed that a correspondent, in a very agreeable and readable letter, confessed that himself and companion fired into the body of a covey. Fie on him! where are his modesty and sporting reputation—first, to commit so gross an outrage, and secondly, to blazon it to the world? Does he not know that for one bird he bags in this ignoble manner, several will go off wounded, to die a lingering death, or, crippled, fall a prey to the first filthy buzzard or rapacious hawk that comes across him? Gentlemen, when you shoot, think of this, and do not uselessly destroy the precious gifts of an ever-bountiful Providence.

The majority of the last family we got possession of, and ere noon had arrived, had seventy head of prairie chicken fairly bagged.

Hank selected a well-suited place for our meal, and with *otium cum dignitate* we passed the meridian hours of the day, happy and contented, at peace with all men, and conscious of the pleasure of successfully following an innocent pursuit.

We remained under the hedge till after two o'clock, eating, chatting, and smoking, the irrepressible Hank relating, in the most facetious manner, several most amusing anecdotes of his previous career. One story in particular caused me to laugh more than ever I remember to have done, saving the night that a Dutchman told me a yarn of his first experience of a wasps' nest; but as the western sun commenced to elongate its shadows, and the afternoon breeze began to cool the atmosphere, a start was agreed upon, and with one accord each rose and shouldered his gun, intent on doing good shooting and further swelling the capacity of our already distended game-bags. The fresh brace of dogs were uncoupled, and, amid the discordant notes and piteous whining of our discarded morning favourites, we started for the beat.

The ground we were about to hunt exactly resembled in appearance and vegetation what we had traversed in the morning, and our anticipations of sport, from former experience, were up to the boiling-point. However, we must have walked quite an hour before either obtained a shot, although the slut ran up two birds, for which she got a severe rating. In prairie chicken-shooting I have frequently observed, and on this occasion it was a corroboration of the fact, that during the heat of mid-day, or immediately afterwards, pinnated grouse are seldom or never to be found near cultivation; why, I cannot say, but they always appear in an unaccountable manner to have transferred themselves to the uninterrupted prairie.

Our lengthened tramp had now brought us to ground more irregular, with vegetation more rank, and sparsely sprinkled with dwarf osier and willow, the surface being damp, and occasionally intersected with rivulets. Our spirits were all becoming depressed from our want of success, and even a new beat had been proposed, and was on the eve of being accepted, when both our canines stood, not ten yards apart, and each, apparently, on different birds. This pleasing incident revived our drooping spirits, and with steady, regular stride we approached the dogs. As we got to them, three birds flushed, which were immediately cut down; still another, and another, met the same fate; and in less than five minutes nine were on the ground. These were without difficulty retrieved, and the dogs ordered on to find more; scarce a hundred yards had they ranged when they a second time found game, the slut leading and the dog just at her shoulder, backing. It was perfectly evident that we had found the retreat of the prairie chickens: water or solitude had undoubtedly caused them to assemble here. The prairie fowl, although partial, at some seasons and portion of the day, to damp ground, I believe do not drink like the majority of other birds, but simply pick off the minute globules of dew that adhere to the grasses. This I know from my own personal observation, and accounts for the difficulty of keeping this species alive in a state of captivity. The majority of persons having them in confinement would undoubtedly place a cup of water in their cages, little imagining that scattering the moisture over some grass would be the way most acceptable.

Soon we got to the dogs, and never in the course of my experience did I see a sharper half hour's work. Bird after bird rose, and was knocked over; scarcely had we time to thrust into the breeches fresh cartridges before we were called upon to deliver our fire; not less than a hundred and fifty birds must have been flushed in that space of time, out of which number nearly half fell to our guns. At one moment, over twenty were on the ground, waiting to be picked up; and, better than all, we did not lose a single cripple, although one old cock, which had only been pinioned, cost us five minutes before he was placed in the bag. With universal consent we agreed to retrace our steps, and before we reached the conveyance, five more grouse had shared the fate of their fellows. On arriving at the scene of our trencher performances at noon-day, we observed several flocks of duck hovering over a portion of a corn-field in the vicinity, and as the day had still an hour or two before dark, we concluded to try our luck. Cartridges with No. 5 shot were soon substituted for the balance we had left in our pockets, and scattering each in the direction which the bent of his fancy dictated, we sought the friendly cover of the giant cornstalks. Progressing slowly and cautiously, prepared for aught that chance should throw in my way, on casting my eyes to the left, I perceived I was near the edge of a small sheet of water, the margin of which was densely covered with water-lilies. Here, no doubt, was the sanctum of the web-footed gentry; so doubling my back almost in two, and gliding along as carefully as if about to circumvent a buck, I reached the line of demarcation between the grain and the aquatic plants.

Slowly raising my head, the first animate object that struck my vision was the looming, dark figure of a goose, his head under water, carelessly feeding, as if he were perfectly satisfied that his retirement was free from interruption. Self-confident that his fate was in my hands, I complacently waited till he should raise his caput, and I should have the satisfaction of enjoying his surprise. My patience was not long taxed, and a more ridiculous scene you could scarce imagine, for as he raised his long neck, the first thing his eye rested on was the figure of your humble servant; a rush, splutter and honk, and he was fairly on his way, still evidently undecided which direction to choose to avoid danger. Little time, however, I left him for choice, and thirty-five yards did not divide us ere my charge of No. 5 brought him summarily back to the bosom of his liquid home. The echoes had scarce answered my report when dozens of duck were on the wing, and some of them rose so close that it was truly extraordinary that I had not previously seen them; among their number a splendid old green-headed mallard struck my fancy, and my left barrel enabled me to cultivate a closer acquaintance. Soon I had both retrieved, for I had brought one of my setters with me, which was equally good on land or water. On inspection, Mr. Goosey proved remarkably fat, his corpulency possibly being the reason that he had remained behind, and not migrated with his comrades to their northern summer haunts and breeding retreats. How my mouth watered when I thought of the delicacy and flavour of a slice of his plump breast, if properly roasted, not too much done, with a squeeze of fresh lemon over it and a tiny pinch of cayenne pepper, and mentally resolved that his corpus should form the dish of honour on our board at no distant date! On the bank of this pond I determined to wait, convinced that I should not find a better situation for dealing destruction to the much-coveted broad-bills.

What sportsman is there who does not take pleasure in bagging a duck? He may have killed dozens, and examined minutely each, still he does not tire admiring the last; the brilliant plumage, the gorgeous colouring of the neck and head, have charms so deeply seated that it is impossible to satiate the fancy. For about ten minutes no visitors arrived, when a cunning old mallard hove in sight, bearing down direct for my screen, undoubtedly a scout out on observation; lower and lower I cowered as he approached, trusting that the colour of my clothes and the shelter of the corn would prevent his keen eye from perceiving my whereabouts, well aware if I could only fetch him down, his companions would soon follow, as their scout would not return to report unfavourably. On the drake came straight as a line, and was almost within range, when he turned to the left, too far distant to shoot with probable success. "Confound him!" I could not help muttering in disgust at his wildness. However, he continued to fly round in circles, each gradually diminishing in diameter, of which the water formed the centre. Move I dare not, one inch would probably betray me, and I nearly squinted my eyes out of my head, following, as far as possible, his circular flight. At length the wished-for chance arrived, and he presented a fair broadside, about thirty-five yards distant; holding my gun almost two feet in advance, I pressed the trigger, and down he came all of a heap, and almost to the ground; my dog was already on his way to pick him up, when, with a violent effort, the bird recovered himself and commenced slowly at first to rise, quicker and quicker became his ascent. "Why don't you put in your second barrel?" I hear you exclaim. Well, simply for this reason, that I had already commenced loading, and the whole performance was so unexpected that I lost my self-possession. Higher and higher he went, almost perpendicularly, as if he were bound for a trip to the clouds. Watching, with straining eyes, his extraordinary performances, feeling fully convinced he was hit in the head, I suddenly perceived him turn on his back, and if his ascent had been rapid, the descent was doubly so, for, when he struck *terra firma*, the thud that he made was sufficient to indicate, if life had not previously been extinct, it now undoubtedly was.

Soon more stragglers commenced coming in, and the fusilade became constant. Mallard and teal were both worthy game, and as I was shooting well, I soon had a large number at my feet. Nor did duck alone pay me a visit, several prairie chickens, on their way for their evening feed, bit the dust; and just as I thought it was high time for retiring, Hank's stentorian voice was heard summoning stragglers, the team being already hitched, and he impatient to be *en route* for the settlement. Fifteen duck and five prairie chickens were the result of little over an hour's shooting, and that without moving five yards to the right or left, and better still, without getting a wet foot.

CHAPTER IX.

MOOSE DEER.
(*Cervus Alces.*)

I NEVER think of the State of Maine without the most intense feelings of pleasure, for there among the pine-clad hills and wood-embosomed lakes I have enjoyed many, many weeks and months so free from care, so productive of pleasure, that the recollection can never pass away; but these pleasures are not without alloy. Alas! that we should grow old, and the companions whose society we dearly cherished should be no more, and that he in whom all our confidence had been centred, and whose society we loved, should in his youth be summoned to occupy a soldier's grave!

A truce to these painful reminiscences. Moose deer and moose hunting is the subject; sentiment we will leave to the poet or the love-sick schoolboy.

The State of Maine is characterised by the numerous labyrinths of lakes that are scattered over it in every direction, divided from each other by mountainous ridges, clothed to their summits with giant pine trees and the many varieties of hard woods peculiar to these latitudes, alike giving beauty to the landscape and affording food and shelter for every kind of Northern game. On the extensive flat meadows that edge these lakes or form the margin of many of the numerous noble rivers, in the hollows, ravines and hill-sides, will the moose deer's home be found, his choice of quarters being regulated by the changes of the seasons. New Brunswick and Nova Scotia also are favourite resorts of this giant deer. In these provinces he still remains numerous; but in northern New Hampshire, Vermont, and north-eastern New York State, where, a quarter of a century since, moose were plentiful, I doubt if at the present date a single specimen can be found. Such is the result of civilisation and the influx of the white man.

The size to which the moose deer grows has been variously stated. Audubon says over twenty hands; Mr. Hays, an animal artist of great talent, and who has spent many years studying his profession in the native haunts of all the subjects he has used his brush upon, informs me that he has known animals to grow much larger. From this gentleman's experience as a hunter and naturalist, I have not the slightest doubt that he is correct. However, I believe about sixteen and a half hands to be the average height of a full-grown male, and that certain localities—possibly where greater abundance of the most suitable food is to be found—produce much larger animals. All the moose that I have heard of being killed in Labrador—where the winters are particularly severe and vegetation sparse—have been smaller than those shot in the State of Maine; nor can I see any reason to doubt such being the case. We know how other genera are affected by such local peculiarities, and why should this animal be an exception?

It is the habit of sportsmen and naturalists to praise the appearance of the moose. My own impression is that there is no animal more ungainly, awkward looking, and apparently disproportioned. That he is admirably constructed for the part he has to play in life there is no question, but the very requisites with which he is endowed, give him such an unusual appearance that prejudice alone can call him handsome.

The Virginian deer, the fallow deer, the Wapiti, and the red deer, are, to me, perfect in shape, graceful in their movements, and ornamental to the landscape; but the moose, on the other hand, with his short, thick neck, asinine head, protruding eyes, heavy broad ears, tremendous antlers, long, awkward, powerful legs and disproportionate withers, looking even higher than they are from the mane that surmounts them, can never be considered by an impartial judge but an awkward and clumsy-looking brute.

Of all the ruminants on the American continent, the moose is the tallest. I doubt not that a stall-fed ox can be made to weigh as heavy, but not to attain the stature, and on this account, as well as many others, it is really a duty that the legislatures of the various States of which he is an inhabitant owe to the country at large to pass and enforce such laws as will prevent his ultimate annihilation.

Probably it may never again be my good fortune to revisit America; but can I ever forget the happy days and nights I have spent in the dense swamp, sparsely covered, barren, tangled wood-land, or over the brilliant camp-fire, when, miles and miles away from civilisation, I have been on an expedition to hunt moose? No! Though I have shot in all parts of the world, gone through scenes exciting, both as soldier and hunter, Northern Maine, with all its glorious lakes, rivers, and mountains, will stand paramount: for there my experience of moose hunting was gained; there I made my maiden effort, which was a failure, to return years afterwards and awake the echoes with the war-whoop that proclaims success.

In December, moose deer cast their horns; by April, the successors commence to sprout; by the end of June full form is developed, but not till many weeks later are they denuded of velvet; when that takes place the horns are perfectly white, but exposure to the atmosphere soon gives them a tawny shade, which deepens with the lapse of time. The cow, of course, never bears these ornaments, but the young bull-calf at one year throws out a brace of knobs an inch in length; in the second season these are about six inches long; the third year the antlers increase to nine or ten inches, with a fork. In the fourth season palmation is exhibited with several points. From this age there is a gradual increase in the palmation and number of points till the animal attains its greatest vigour, from which period the horns decrease in width and weight, at the same time becoming more elongated. Twenty-three is the greatest number of points I have seen on one head, and the weight of the horns just exceeded seventy pounds. I doubt if larger has ever, of late years, been found.

The young moose deer, that is, those under five years, frequently do not show their new head-dress till March. Instances have been known—still, I have no doubt that such were great exceptions—of young males bearing the old horns as late as the calving season, which is in the end of April, and in Labrador and far northern localities, May.

In September the rutting season commences. Then is the period to see this great animal in all the magnificence of his strength. Reckless and furious he rushes about, bellowing forth defiance to his own sex, and what is accepted as notes of love by the other. Woe betide the traveller, the unarmed or inexperienced man who should then meet him, if no place of safety is at hand, for nought but their total destruction would be the result. I knew an instance where a French Canadian nearly lost his life by one of these furious beasts. He had gone with his pony and sled to bring a boat across a portage, and on his return, while threading the intricacies of the bush-path, a moose, excited with rage and lust, rushed past him. Indiscreetly he fired a charge of small shot after the retreating termagant, which brought him to the right-about, and caused him to charge. Into the boat jumped the Canadian, but the thin ribs and planks afforded no protection from such an assailant. The frail craft was soon knocked to pieces, and our friend took to a tree, when, from his perch, he witnessed his pony gored and trampled to death. Moral: Don't fire small shot at moose if you have any regard for your life.

During the rutting season many bull moose are

annually killed, for the hunters, taking advantage of their then combative disposition, secrete themselves, and imitate, by means of a roll of birch bark, the challenge note of an excited male. Some gallant lord of the wilderness hears the false, deceptive call, and, believing that his demesne has been invaded by a rival, towering with rage, he rushes in the direction whence the sound proceeds, intent on repelling the invader. Listening to the repeated calls, again and again the bull answers, till at length he is drawn within the range of the rifle of the secreted hunter. My maiden effort at moose shooting was made in such a manner. As if it were but yesterday, the whole adventure is written plainly on my memory. I had only been in America a few months. The attractions of Saratoga I could not avoid, and when there became acquainted with a family of St. Francis Indians, earning a precarious subsistence by basket-making. Before this I had never met any of the aborigines of the American continent, and hour after hour I passed idling around their encampment, listening to stories of the chase, and more especially of moose hunting. The darkskinned race got my spare pocket-money, and I in return all their knowledge of woodcraft that could be theoretically imparted. The spirit of adventure had become excited within me, and ere I left Saratoga I had faithfully promised to visit St. Francis in autumn, to join one of my new acquaintances in a moose hunt.

The beautiful tints of an American autumn were in their greatest brilliancy when I reached the termination of a long and tedious journey to accept the proffered hospitalities. My reception was not so enthusiastic as I expected; in fact, my ardour was a little damped by the marked coolness of my host. Yet, after coming such a distance, I was determined to do some hunting, and a well-stocked purse enabled me to carry out my wishes. Starting at early morning, on a beautiful clear day, we descended a stream, a tributary of the Penobscot River, for eight or ten hours. The easy motion of the birch bark, the grand scenery and the brilliant coloured foliage, recalled many a vision I had formed of what fairyland must resemble. About four o'clock we disembarked, our birch bark was shouldered, and a portage of a mile or two traversed, when the margin of a clear, calm lake was reached, surrounded with beautiful green hills. Soon again we were on the bosom of the waters, arriving at a second halting-place as the sun in glorious splendour dipped the western horizon. Hiding the frail canoe in some brush, my attendant leading, we started up an acclivity, when, after an hour's rough and difficult walking, the Indian stopped and sounded a note on his birch-bark horn.

To this there was no response, but my friend assured me, "Plenty moose by-by."

The night was as beautiful as the day preceding it. The hunter's moon was at its full, and near objects could be seen almost as distinctly as when the sun was high in the heavens. Several efforts with the call had been made; disappointment and failure began to appear certain, when a distant and unknown sound struck my ear. At the same moment the redskin seized my arm and whispered, "Old bull." We both placed ourselves in a hemlock tree, and numerous were the injunctions I received of the necessity of silence. Afraid to move, cramped in an awkward position, for near a mortal hour I endured the torments, certainly not of the blessed; still move I would not, ultimately could not, as the answering voice of the bull in response to the Indian's call told that the giant was rapidly approaching. At length—oh, how glad I was!—the noblest fellow I had ever set eyes upon broke into the opening at a gentle trot, stopped and impatiently stamped his foot. The distance that the game was from us could not have been more than thirty yards. Slowly and imperceptibly the Indian's gun was getting into shooting position. I attempted to do the same with mine, when —oh! what excuse can I offer?—bang went the right barrel, and, but for a vigorous effort, I should have fallen from my perch.

I had better draw a veil over the recriminations that ensued, for homicide was nearly the result, whether justifiable or not must be for others to decide; but St. Francis was not long honoured with my presence. Of moose hunting I had seen enough for one season, and for many a year not even my bosom friends knew that I had ever made an attempt on such a large class of game.

In the close, warm weather of July and August this game is much pestered with flies. To avoid these plagues, the moose almost becomes aquatic in his habits; for hours he will completely submerge himself, with nought but his head above the surface. At this season their principal food is the long, succulent limbs and leaves of the water lily. In the tributary streams that help to feed Moosehead Lake it is no uncommon thing for the fisherman or tourist, on his aquatic excursions, to come across moose floating, or see them reach the shore in advance of him, as the wary animals have been alarmed, either by voices or the wind. Such was my fortune once when fishing in a tributary of Lake Parmacheney. Trout had all day been on the feed; my gun lay carelessly at my feet, half buried in blankets and other hunter's paraphernalia, in the bottom of my canoe, which I had permitted silently to drift with the current. Suddenly I heard a splash, as if all the fish in the river had collected to make a simultaneous rise; but, instead of fin, it was fur, and a splendid moose, bearing a noble set of antlers, plunged through the weeds, and soon disappeared in the recesses of the forest. If I had been prepared, or even had my gun been obtainable at a moment's notice, I could with ease have administered the *coup de grâce*.

When the season advances, and the sparse advent snows occasionally give warning that winter is at hand, the moose deer leave the morass and river banks for higher ground. Here they collect in families, previous to yarding, which takes place as soon as the lands of these Northern wilds have received their annual deep and pure white covering. At this time the moose lives in comparative security, his length of limb and tremendous power enabling him to defy all pursuers. Enjoy well thy rest—enjoy it, I say, for it is but for a short season: for when the sun again warms the landscape, and a crust becomes formed through the thaw by day and frost of night, you will require more than that superhuman power to save you from the persevering Indian or venturous white man. Poor creature! your chance when once pursued, when a heavy crust is formed, is indeed small. I know no denizen of the forest that, at any period of life, has the odds so fearfully against him.

As may be imagined, the end of February and March are the periods when the greatest havoc among these animals takes place, and I regret to say that frequently the fiendish love of carnage alone seems to occupy the mind of the pursuer. I have known instances—I grieve to say many—when moose have been killed simply for the sake of killing; for, with the exception of one or two titbits, the giant carcass has been left to satiate the appetite of the wild beasts of the forest. If one who has been guilty of such unjustifiable conduct should read this, let his conscience reproach him for the past, and the sting of remorse cause him to resolve never to be again an offender.

The exact position of the scene which I am about to describe I will not name. Gentle reader, say not that I am selfish: for probably never again shall I fire a shot upon it; but my well-tried friend and hunting companion visits it still each year, and, as he introduced me to its well-stocked grounds, I had no hesitation, when last we parted, in pledging my word to keep my knowledge from the world. Suffice it to say, that it lies within the limits of the State of Maine.

The days that had heralded the advent of March

had been extremely warm, the nights clear, with sharp frost; just such weather as would be pronounced first-class for the collecting of sap to make maple sugar. Two days' journey had been required to bring us to the desired locality, for we had both agreed that no search for moose should be made till a favourite neighbourhood alike beautiful in summer or winter was reached. Moreover, here we should find a log hut, erected two seasons previously, and which we had every reason to believe would be in a thorough state of repair. In due course of time we arrived at our rendezvous; the snow was cleared out of the structure, and, considering all things, the two Penobscot Indians who accompanied us succeeded in making our temporary residence look more than inviting. The first night passed in the usual manner; we each pledged the other's health more than once, and again and again the pipes required filling. Still we slept soundly, and day had well broken before either turned out. A hurried cup of coffee and a few morsels of cold meat and biscuit sufficed for breakfast, so that ere the sun had risen over the neighbouring hill we were *en route* for the scene of action. The country that we traversed was covered with hard wood, but not densely crowded —so open, in fact, that a fair shot would severely have punished woodcock which had taken shelter in a similar locality. After tramping three miles, the Indians leading, and I causing much amusement by a succession of catastrophes from one snow-shoe overlapping the other, a halt was made, and the expression of the guide spoke plainly of the vicinity of game; without questioning, we turned off to the left, still following in single file. Stooping low and slowly advancing for some moments, we came upon a yard—but, alas! deserted; but such had not been long the case. Our dark-skinned companions were jubilant; visions of moose meat floated before them, and straight they directed their steps to the place of exit, for the occupants had winded us earlier than expected. To a novice but one track appeared, yet the Indians held up their four fingers to indicate that that had been the number of inmates. Soon we found their information correct; for, after a pursuit of an hour and a half, we perceived our game—a bull, cow, and two calves—going over a neighbouring swell. The reason of this deceptive appearance of the trail is caused by the male leading, and the cow and calves in succession stepping as nearly as possible in the footsteps of their predecessors.

Just as we supposed ourselves on the verge of success, the pursued passed through a second yard, easily known by the trampled state of the snow and barked sides of the trees. The occupants of this retreat had joined those we were following. This additional force to the pursued added fresh excitement to the chase, and the distress resulting from pace was for the time forgotten. In an hour more we were again in view, and soon afterwards among the game. My companions I will leave to themselves, and confine myself to my own performance. One of the males had a noble head of horns. These I determined to be possessed of; so, marking him for mine, I resolved not to halt till successful. Again and again I thought that but a few minutes would elapse till I could shoot; but either from the snow being less deep, or the animal making extra efforts, at least an hour had elapsed before the quarry was sufficiently close to deliver with precision a fatal shot.

Soon I was joined by one of the Indians, then by the others. Four moose had been killed; so my companion and self agreed that we had reaped enough reward for one day's work. Next day was equally successful, and more game was seen than on the first essay. I doubt not if we had been so minded, for days we might have continued this slaughter; but, as it was, we had as much meat as we could transport to the settlement.

A more rapid manner of taking moose when there

is a crust, and one much practised, is to be accompanied by a small, active dog, which, if properly trained to his work, will never lay hold, but only snap at the quarry's heels. The poor moose is thus soon brought to bay; but his active pursuer, whose weight is so light that he does not break through the crust, dances around him scatheless, snapping at every momentarily exposed point, and so engaging the victim's attention that the hunter can approach the game sufficiently close to deliver with certainty an unfailing shot.

The flesh of the moose, although sweet, is very coarse. Still, many people prefer it to all other. I cannot say that such is the case with me, good beef being to my idea infinitely superior. The tongue, last entrail, and especially the mouffle or extremity of the upper lip, are great delicacies, more particularly when eaten cooked in the primitive style of the backwoods. It may be the wood fire, it may be the want of seasoning, or more probably still the fresh air and severe exercise of the hunt; but all that I have eaten when snugly housed about a camp-fire has been relished with additional gusto. A *bonne bouche* which must not be forgotten, and which only the moose hunter can enjoy, or those who live near the haunts of this animal, is the marrow from the shank-bones of the legs, cooked immediately after the animal is killed. This, served on toast, with a sprinkling of cayenne pepper, would make the mouth of the most fastidious epicure water, if he had previous experience of its excellence.

The moose deer changes much in appearance with the rotations of the seasons. In summer the coat is short and fine; in winter coarse and long. Underneath the hair is found an abundant crop of soft wool, which doubtless enables them to endure the greater severity of the northern winters. The face-hair, different from that of the horse or cow, grows upwards from the mouffle, on the termination of which there is a triangular bare spot. The power of the jaws and teeth of the moose is very great. The facility with which they strip the bark from those trees that constitute their favourite food is wonderful. Their pace is either a walk or trot, the usual bounding gait of other species being unknown to them. Even if a fallen tree interrupt their progress, instead of rising at it like a horse, they manage to clamber over in a most effective manner.

Not far from Trois Rivieres, in Canada, I heard of a moose deer being broken in for saddle purposes. The truth of this I am more than sceptical about. I have also been informed that a brace were broken for harness, and that long and well they performed their part, being possessed of immense powers of draught. This latter report does not to me appear so improbable as the former.

Two methods of capturing moose I have not alluded to,—for why? They appear so antagonistic to all those feelings that should actuate the gentleman; viz., by snaring, and immense steel spring traps. The minutiæ of the modes of proceeding by which the unsuspicious game is induced to enter either of the above devices, I am certain would not be interesting to a sportsman.

For many years it was a disputed point whether the moose deer of America and the elk of Europe were the same species; but the most eminent of recent and present authorities agree that they are identical. Captain Hardy, of the Royal Artillery, who was stationed many years in Canada, and devoted much of his time to moose hunting, as well as studying this animal's habits, and who is also conversant with the European elk, in the admirable articles which he has published in that deservedly esteemed periodical on practical natural history—*Land and Water*—emphatically asserts that there are not the smallest grounds for any diversity of opinion on the subject. Audubon, an authority second to none, refuses to give a decision, and justly so, for he was not conversant with the European animal.

His Royal Highness the Prince of Wales has a brace of Scandinavian elks at his country residence, Sandringham. They are both rising two years in age. If any of our naturalists will take the trouble to inspect them, doubtless they will concur in the decision of Captain Hardy.

CHAPTER X.

SHOOTING IN ILLINOIS.

AFTER having eaten a good dinner, changed my wet clothes for dry, and made all comfortable for the evening,—not even gun-washing to trouble me,—as I whiff my glowing pipe, I feel in good fellowship with all the world; and only desire, to complete the enjoyment of the past day, "to fight my battles o'er again." Some may smile at what they think a feather-bed sportsman's fancy, but among the most ardent Nimrods the retrospect of the day's sport has always caused almost as much pleasure as the actual performance. Who that has been out in the open air from morning till night, probably with damp or even wet feet, has not felt and enjoyed the luxury of warm slippers, dry socks, and invigorating ablutions? Yes, gentle reader, as I sip the juice of the grape, inhale the fumes of the fragrant weed, and recline comfortably in my arm-chair, I feel how much I have reason to thank the Creator for the blessings He has so bounteously showered upon me. But to our work:—The first day's partridge (*Perdrix Virginiensis*) shooting of the season is past, and, like all its predecessors, is numbered with days gone by, one sole peculiarity marking it; namely, that the birds, generally speaking, were larger, stronger, and more numerous than I ever remember seeing them. The weather, too, could not have been more appropriate; bright, clear, and bracing, with just sufficient wind and dampness to make the scent good. Although, the previous evening, 7 A.M. was the hour appointed for breakfast, and all promised most faithfully to be present at that time, it was fully an hour later before the muster-roll could be read over without finding absentees. Perhaps the cause of this remissness may be indicated by repeated calls for brandy and soda-water at an early hour, a demand which, if I remember aright, is always more than ominous. However, by a few minutes after nine we left the house, and, with many a pungent joke and sharp repartee, entered the belt of woodland that divided us from the prairie.

At this season (October),* who, that has the slightest

* In the majority of States partridge shooting commences on the 1st October sense of colour in his composition, can fail to admire the manifold shades and tintings of the foliage during an American autumn? True, the change of colour denotes decay and departing glory; still the richness and brilliancy of the numerous hues have far from a depressing effect. The European poets have sung of autumn in strains so sad that one can scarce read their effusions without getting the dolefuls; perhaps this arises from their landscape lacking the brilliant hues of the sumach, maple, and Virginia creeper, which contrast so magnificently with the less radiant oak or beech, or the intensely green pine and hemlock. There is but one period of the year that can compare, in my humble opinion, with the Fall, and that only in the Western States. I allude to that portion of the spring when the snow-white dogwood and refulgent pink-bud are in the full possession of their delicate and lovely blossom. A quarter of a mile brought us to the edge of our intended beat, and as the faithful and keen-scented setters were uncoupled, we individually felt luck was on our side, and in all human probability we should have first-class sport. Soon our guns received the correct quantity of ammunition, and while Sancho and Don were down at "charge," the lively sound of the ramrod, or the sharp, clear clicking of the locks, as each half-cocked his gun, announced the determination of all to do their best to give a good account of the first unfortunate covey we should come across. Like a general of old or modern times, I mustered my forces in line, and, as if skirmishing, advanced on the still invisible foe. Lawrence County, Illinois, where we were, is eminently suited for partridge shooting, and from its open nature, clear shots are generally offered. Therefore, there is not so much credit due to the sportsman who kills nearly every shot, as there would be in the Eastern States, where the piece of ground the least accessible is the most probable on which to find game.

Well, the dogs were uncoupled, and the guns loaded, and forward we rapidly advanced over the elastic turf, happy in our anticipated pleasure, brimful of energy and expectation. Our two canines, which had not been hunted lately, quartered their ground in splendid style, laying down to their gallop like thoroughbreds, and anxiously sniffing the pure atmosphere, in hope of inhaling the taint emitted by that most beautiful bird, and one perfectly adapted for the sportsman's amusement, the American partridge. I am aware that many will question this assertion, and perhaps bring volumes of argument to prove that I am wrong; but, at the risk of the charge of obstinacy, I trust I shall be pardoned if I retain my opinion. We were not long kept unemployed, for on the edge of a corn-field, where the briers occupied an uninterrupted space, both Sancho and Don set. With considerable difficulty I restrained the ardour of my companions; one in particular, who seemed always to regard it as a matter of life and death to get as soon as possible within shooting distance, and invariably missed his birds after all. We soon reached the staunch dogs, nor were we kept long waiting, for a sudden whirr showed us the entire family on the wing, and every barrel vomited forth its intended fatal contents. Four birds fell, two being claimed by G., without quibble, and the remaining duo I felt confident were mine; at least, never was my gun held straighter, or my aim more deliberate; still, T., our impatient friend, emphatically declared that one of them was a victim to his prowess. To dispute the point I deemed unnecessary and unbecoming, for I was host; so without further words, and I trust with becoming dignity, I relinquished the claim of possession, although I could not help thinking it really strange that my hand and eye should so suddenly have lost their cunning, beside having that internal conviction, which we all possess, of having made good shots. Our quarry was rapidly brought to bag, and the balance of the persecuted family was followed. Instead of their making for the timber, or the brush which grew upon its edge, they had flown out, perhaps a couple of hundred yards farther, into the prairie, where there was nothing to cause a deviation in their flight, or prevent our obtaining clear and uninterrupted aim.

The splendid chance thus presented of filling our game bags was greedily accepted and acted upon. Don found the beauties in a few minutes, and Sancho stealthily approached his brother with cautious step, frequently stopping and backing with praiseworthy zeal. The partridge* on this occasion were more difficult to force on the wing, and nearly all got up singly. One circumstance, however, I noted, that although G. and self did clean work, our friend T. failed on both occasions. But undoubtedly this was the result of accident, as he informed us that one barrel hung fire and the other exploded just at the moment that the bird had made a sudden alteration in its flight. I could not help commiserating with him at these untoward circumstances, and felt almost irate with G. (who was an old friend and former shooting chum of T.'s), for heartlessly laughing at his friend's

---

* This bird has the extraordinary power of withholding its scent, which it frequently does for ten or fifteen minutes after lighting.

mishaps. Finally four birds flushed, and six barrels again spoke, the quarto falling simultaneously with the report. Scarcely had they touched the ground when T. informed us with evident satisfaction that he had got his hand in now, as two of the last victims could well attest. However, on picking up the game, what was my surprise when a bird I felt confident was mine was a second time claimed; nor was this all: G. vowed he had killed both of his; still T. equally energetically disputed his success, and would not listen to anything to the contrary; moreover he offered to prove, and in truth did with logic and argument worthy of the bench, how he was undoubtedly the proper proprietor.

We are all aware that strange coincidences take place in the hunting-field—so very strange that the narration of them suggests a liberal draft on the imagination. I felt willing to attribute these incidents to this source; so thinking a great deal and saying very little, we resumed our labours. Only one bird out of the first lot had escaped, and his flight was in the direction we intended proceeding, so that the chances were all in our favour of picking him up. Again we spread into line, and the well-bred dogs parcelled their ground off as systematically as a merchant's clerk would measure off goods. As we advanced, T., who was on the right flank, with your humble servant in the centre, walked-up the sole survivor of the now decimated family. The bird sprang from his very feet, and both barrels in rapid succession greeted its departure; still Mr. Partridge did not fall, nor did I see the slightest appearance of its having suffered inconvenience. T., however, assured us that it was badly hit and would fall immediately, requesting us to mark it well, as he much desired to get it, in order to see where it was struck, and "how the mischief" it did not drop at once. We all strained our optics, at least I did, till my sight was almost obscured by liquid, so earnest was I to gratify my friend's wishes; but, alas! the bird was possessed of a most unusual amount of vitality, and ultimately vanished, apparently going stronger than when it started. T. then appealed to G., if he did not see the feathers fly, and when he answered in the negative, my opinion was demanded; however, I was loth to confess that the only feathers flying I was aware of, were those that assisted the bird in ridding himself of such dangerous neighbours and getting as far from our vicinity as possible. In fact, I was commencing to "smell a mice," as the Dutchman said, and thought our worthy, energetic friend much resembled Mr. Jogglebury Crowdey, the gentleman whose acquaintance Mr. Sponge made in his "sporting tour," and there certainly was a strong likeness in more than one way.

I will submit the description, and let my friends see if I had not just grounds for coming to this conclusion. "Jog had had many a game at romps with these birds, and knew their haunts and habits to a nicety. The covey consisted of thirteen originally, but by repeated blazings into the 'broun of 'em' he had succeeded in knocking down two. Jog was not one of your conceited shots who never fired but when he was sure of killing; on the contrary, he always let drive far or near, and even if he shot a hare, which he sometimes did with the first barrel, he always popped the second into her to make sure. Jog's shooting afforded amusement to the neighbourhood. On one occasion, a party of reapers having watched him miss twelve shots in succession, gave him three cheers on coming to the thirteenth."

Our worthy friend T. was the greatest theoretical sportsman I ever met, and to hear him talk you would imagine that he had reduced the whole performance to such a certainty, that to let a bird get off "scot free" was unknown to his double-barrel when he had the pulling of the triggers.

On one occasion, when on a shooting expedition, he dropped into a tavern the evening before commencing operations. The room was full of loungers, many of whom were good shots, and were to accompany our friend on the morrow. Shooting soon became the absorbing subject of conversation, and so admirably did T. blow and expatiate on his skill—explaining and proving, in the most scientific manner, how every man, no matter what his infirmities, might become a perfect crack—that the listeners got scared, and preferred remaining at home to being beaten by a "city gent."

Our day terminated with a heavy bag, and my friend T. to this day enjoys among his circle of acquaintances the reputation of being the very best theoretical, and the very worst practical, sportsman in the State of Ohio.

CHAPTER XI.

BLACK BEAR.

(*Ursus Americanus.*)

NONE of the *feræ naturæ* are better known in a state of captivity than the black bear. What village schoolboy, however remote the hamlet in which he resides, cannot remember poor Bruin being led round by some half-washed, uncombed foreigner, or his forming a portion of the attractions which drew the gaping crowd to enter the strong-smelling precincts of the annually-visiting erratic menagerie? Alas! hard is the poor bear's life when he is thus a prisoner. In summer he is kept on half diet, and shut up in a miserable den; in winter he is stowed away in a cellar, and possibly, at least once a week, baited with curs, that the blackguard owner may raise enough funds to carry on his vagrant, idle life. How different this from the life the bear enjoyed in his native woods, wandering about at pleasure, enjoying every luxury of nature that the season produces; and, if in a country subject to a severe winter, quietly sleeping through that portion of the year when the winds, loaded with frost and snow, whistle round his snug retreat! The black bear at one period was very widely distributed over the North American continent. Its range now, on account of the advance and increase of population, has been much restricted; still, wherever there are large tracks of uncultivated ground, representatives of this species will be found, whether in Canada or Labrador, Florida, Georgia, or the Far West, until you reach the Rocky Mountains, beyond which I have never heard of the black bear being seen, the cinnamon bear (*Ursus cinnamomus*) and the grizzly bear (*Ursus ferox*) there supplying his place. So numerous still are the black bears in some parts of the United States that a portion of each year is set aside by the squatters and farmers for their capture, and large packs of curs, specially trained to assist, are kept for this purpose; and numerous instances are on record of thirty, or even forty bears having in a couple of months fallen before one hunter's rifle. The flesh, which is with justice much prized, is either salted down or smoked for future use; while the pelt furnishes a bed, or is sold to the traders, ultimately to be made into rugs for sleighs or the coarser kinds of furs for women and children.

The different sizes to which black bears attain in various sections of the country are somewhat remarkable; so much so that I have often been induced to believe that they were entitled at least to be considered varieties, but otherwise they are so similar in habits of life, choice of food, and residence, that it would only be opening a path that might lead to innumerable intricacies without the probability of resulting in benefit. The black bear of Michigan, Wisconsin, and the regions bordering on these States, never exceeds two hundred and fifty pounds; these are generally denominated hog bear; but when you descend the Mississippi and get into the canebrakes of Arkansas, numbers are annually killed that reach four hundredweight. Coming eastward, you find a still larger animal, and I have heard from undoubted sources that in the State of Maine; and along the edges of New Brunswick, six, or even seven hundred pounds' weight is no unusual size for bears to attain. Doubtless these differences are occasioned by varieties or abundance of food that the different regions produce, not temperature or climate, as the difference between the latitude of Wisconsin and Maine is very trifling.

Without further preamble, I will attempt a description. The bear is very short in carcass, with an unusually baggy, slack look; the legs are long and powerful in their sweep, and the animal can handle them with the skill and proficiency of a professed pugilist; the head is very nearly an equilateral triangle, with the nose for an apex; the ears are small and rounded, the same distance in situation behind the eye that the eye is from the nose; the measurement in circumference close in front of the shoulder is almost as great as behind, which gradually increases as it ranges backwards till the loftiest point of the spinal vertebræ is reached; while the hind limbs, from their immense muscular power, as well as abundance of flesh, appear like the extremities of a man encased in pegtop trousers. In walking the toes of the fore feet are turned in, while the use of the nether limbs is so human as to appear like a burlesque on *genus homo;* but if a casual observer be thus struck, the anatomist or student of nature recognises in this exaggerated formation the means supplied by nature to ascend trees, escape enemies, or earn its support. The colour when the pelt is prime is glossy black, but in early spring a rufous tint is strongly developed; this is assisted by the undergrowth of wool becoming elongated, and showing through the coarser black hairs that at other seasons are the only visible covering, unless a close and minute inspection be made.

BLACK BEAR. 129

From the eyes in a straight line almost perpendicular to the nose the fur is brown, with a tip of the same colour sometimes over the eyebrow. At the same time, exceptions, more particularly among those of the North-western States, are to be found which are black to the termination of the olfactory organ.

As a general rule, when this bear is in a state of nature, he is extremely timorous of man, flying from him with a stealth and rapidity almost marvellous; but wound him, hurt him, even insult his dignity, and the huntsman may be prepared for a conflict that will only terminate in death; for, once enraged and drawn into conflict, his combativeness increases, never lessening till life is extinct. However, instances have been known where Bruin has not had these excuses for commencing hostilities. Either an old cub engaged with her progeny in imparting to them her extensive knowledge of the world, some gallant lover worshipping at the shrine of his devotion, or scarceness of provisions and desire of gaining some certain retreat where appetite could be gratified, have been the exciting causes in rousing their otherwise peaceful temperament.

The first bear I ever shot was doubtless suffering from the last cause. I will narrate the circumstance. In the State of Wisconsin, near Green River, there are situated some beautiful retired sheets of water. These spots had long possessed me with their attractiveness, for game abounded in their vicinity; the scenery was beautiful, and, above all, you were entirely free from man's intrusion. Could it be wondered, then, that seldom a week passed that I did not find time to visit them? Summer had unconsciously glided into autumn, the dark, dense covering of the trees had changed to all the gaudy hues of the rainbow, and the enlarged ripples on the water, and occasional sighings of the wind, predicted that at no distant period another shroud than the green grasses would cover the surface of the earth.

On the day in question when I left my couch immense numbers of wild fowl were seen migrating southward—evident signs that cold weather had made its appearance north. So, hoping possibly to kill a swan, or a scarce specimen of wild duck, I determined to visit my lakes once more ere they were frozen up. At noon, when I started to fulfil my purpose, large flakes of snow were noiselessly descending, but not in sufficient numbers to obliterate my trail. The water reached, the first glance exposed a sight only seen by those who reside beyond the verges of civilisation, where the wild denizens of the air or inhabitants of the land reign supreme. The surface of the water was covered with ducks of every variety;

moving room even looked scarce; still phalanx after phalanx came swooping down before the wind with the well-known velocity that a wild duck's wings command. Quack, quack, quack, went the ducks on the water; a prolonged note from those in the air answered. The three notes were an invitation, the one note a hearty response, as willingly accepting the invitation as the most hospitable host could desire.

A few shots filled my bag, and I seated myself on a rock, regardless alike of snow or wind, to admire and learn the instinct of the animal world. Hour after hour glided on, and night was near as I returned my pipe to my pocket, unfolded my covering from around my gun-locks, and rose to depart. The snow had, in the meantime, obliterated my path; still the familiar trees and the ever-true-speaking mosses told with certainty the direction. Indolently and self-satisfied I broke into the bush on my homeward route; the weight of the game told heavily on my shoulders. When half of the journey (which I had long wished had been the whole) was reached, I heard a rustling in the brush, evidently caused by large game. Such a warning instantly aroused me, and, on the alert for further sport, I took all the surrounding visible objects in at a glance. In front was a bear. A monster to my vision he appeared, for I was uninitiated at that time—and I believe the eye has a trick of dealing in the marvellous with unaccustomed objects—and, to my horror, Bruin was coming directly towards me. My first feeling was to fly; next, to ascend a tree; thirdly, to disappear into my boots. The second glance gave me more assurance. Mr. Bear was evidently on urgent private affairs; his whole manner bespoke this; and he did not see me; so I determined to stand still, hoping he would remain ignorant of my presence, or, at least, give me a fair show, if compelled to fight. Onward advanced Bruin; closer and closer he came, and the nearer he approached the farther my heart went into my mouth. Still he was fifty yards off, and had plenty of time to change his course; but no such change took place; for if he had been a ball bowled at a wicket the precision of his course could not have been truer. Twenty yards could not have intervened between us when my presence became known, and the manner of welcome I received was far from encouraging, for he halted, sniffed in the air, and gave an angry growl. I wished myself at home in bed, or at the antipodes, or in any place but my present standpoint. For remember, reader, my gun was only loaded with duck shot; and I was green, and, I fear, very soft. It was evident that my appearance was not intimidating, for my adversary neither swerved to right nor left, and his wicked eyes blazed forth flashes of malignant hate. Eight or ten yards more the distance was diminished, when, whether from fear, certain that my last moments had arrived, or knowledge of animals' habits, I gave a shout,—a feeble one, of no distinct note, I believe; but the result was fortunate, for the foe halted, and really seemed uncomfortable, occasionally glancing around, as if he believed retreat, if possible, would be advisable; but second thoughts are not always best. The irresolution was fatal, and the bear found it so ultimately, for he again advanced towards me. When scarcely eight yards divided us, a second shout brought him again to a halt, and, as he sat up, displaying his teeth—symptoms that too truly said, "I will teach you a lesson"—I let him have the contents of the right barrel, aimed for the nose, well knowing the shortness of range would throw the projectiles up. And so it did. At so short a distance the concussion was irresistible; both eyes were destroyed, the forehead up to the apex of the crown fearfully cut up, and the poor bear rolled over, clawing the injured parts in life's last agony. Without hesitation I delivered the *coup de grâce* by discharging the second barrel at the butt of Bruin's ear, thus surely putting a finishing touch to his earthly career. This bear weighed about two hundred and twenty pounds, and was, in the vicinity where killed, deemed a very large one.

When in the State of Maine I was called from my writing by the landlord of the small roadside hotel at which I was residing. He informed me that a bear had entered the clearing,* evidently with the intention of attacking his drove of sheep. Seizing my unloaded gun, and hastily charging both barrels with bullets, I rushed down to join him, bootless as I had been sitting. From an eminence a few yards from the house we took a survey; no bear could be seen; but the timid sheep were huddled in a fence corner, evidently having suffered no ordinary fright.

With anxious gaze we scanned the enclosure; every moment a blackened, charred stump, the memento of some giant monarch of the forest, was mistaken for the bear. Again and again our mistake was found out, and a new object was metamorphosed into a Bruin. Ten minutes were thus spent, the flock of sheep became, if possible, more uneasy, when, with sudden energy, they made a simultaneous dash and crossed to the far side of the field; still no bear was visible, but that he was close at hand was now evident. Loss of time or prolonged suspense began to make us careless; an

* Where the forest has been cut away for cultivation.

advance into the field had even been proposed, and was about to be executed, when the sheep made another start, evidently intent on returning to the position we found them in; but as they passed a log out rushed Bruin, and cut off the retreat of the hindermost. The poor victim made two or three feeble efforts to regain his fellows, then turned and looked his enemy in the face, and from that moment succumbed to fate, at the same time retaining the use of his legs. Nor did Bruin rush up and seize him. He only headed him off when inclined to turn out of the proper direction, driving him all the time towards the right side of the field, which edged on a piece of swamp. Soon the fence was gained; here the sheep's fortitude forsook him, and as both landlord and self had followed as close in rear as advisable, we were witnesses of a proceeding almost incredible. Bruin was evidently in a magnanimous frame of mind, or was overcome by his natural politeness, for without worrying or mauling, never for a moment using his teeth, he picked up the poor sheep between his paws, placed it on the top of the rails, then pushed it over, and with the agility of a greyhound cleared the fence himself. The shock had roused the victim and reanimated him, for both walked off into the bush, the one satisfied to be driven, the other apparently a not over-exacting shepherd. Following up the duo as rapidly and silently as circumstances would permit, we again came on both; but the bear had been annoyed, or the sheep could or would not do what was wanted, for Bruin had seized the unfortunate and dragged him on a log, and was using both teeth and claws with animosity and purpose. Making a stalk I got within twenty yards of both; the sheep's head had already been almost severed, and the hot and liquid gore was evidently giving intense satisfaction to the slayer. With a long steady aim I covered the white horseshoe on the bear's breast; the gun was a large and heavy one, the necessary pressure of the trigger was given, and without a moan, almost without a kick, the would-be despoiler and his prey fell to the earth together. The shot was a good one; the results on dissection proved with what precision and force a solid bullet can be fired from a common shot-gun. This bear weighed four hundred pounds, and, from the decayed and worn teeth, must have been an old stager; in fact, I think age is wanted to give Bruin the courage and desire to attack and kill animal food. The neighbours were soon assembled, my gun was examined and commented on, and I was the hero for the time being.

The white shoe on the breast is commonly, in some sections of the country, the spot which the trapper waits to be exposed, to shoot at. A ball entering there, and going either upwards or horizontally, always proves fatal. However, behind the shoulder, very low down, is the favourite aim with me. In these cross shots, if obtainable, you always have more to shoot at, and the regions of the heart are reached nearer the surface. The butt of the ear, a little backwards, if close enough to make certain, is another deadly point; but the size of this delicate and mortal place is small, and should never be chosen beyond thirty yards. The head shot can, with conical bullets, easily be performed; but a spherical bullet, especially from a small-bore rifle, from the wedge-shape of the cranium, is very apt to glance off without injuring more than the skin.

In hunting bears with dogs, the commonest cur that has pluck enough to snap at his heels is the best animal for the purpose. The bear gets worried, then cross, and ultimately ascends the first tree that his judgment tells him is suitable, resting most frequently on the soonest reached branch out of harm's way, unless the hunter be seen or heard; if so, then the highest foot of bearable timber will be selected. It is not uncommon on these occasions for him to ascend too high for the strength of the limb, when, the bough breaking, both come tumbling to the earth. Although such a rapid and lofty descent would certainly destroy a man, Bruin will arise uninjured, shake himself, and trot off as if nothing had happened.

The vitality of the bear is immense. His powers of destruction when wounded are equally so. So, gentle reader, if it should be your fortune to go bear hunting, pray be careful if you approach them when wounded. A sportsman's maxim, that should never be forgotten, is, "always load your gun before you move from where it was discharged, and never let the temptations or excitement of the moment permit you to hurry when performing this useful duty."

A great many bears have been killed with the knife only, but the person who performs so dangerous a feat must truly be fool-hardy and reckless of consequences, and in my belief such conduct is, except in cases of emergency, most unjustifiable. For one who returns safe in limb and skin from such a contest, the majority who attempt it would be fearfully mauled, or very possibly disabled for life.

The black bear in a state of captivity is extremely restless, and, when old, bad-tempered and treacherous, more especially should he have been teased in his youth; but when he roves the forest, free, he is the laziest and most luxurious fellow, sleeping the greater portion of his time, feeding on nuts or luscious fruits, playing in the sun's heat with comrades, and seldom quarrelling with his brethren. When passages of arms take place, love is the cause, and the battle is waged more in words than blows.

Two or three years ago, in the autumn, about midnight, I was passing through a chain of lakes in the State of Maine; the night was lit by an occasional star, struggling through the rapidly fleeting dark clouds for an opportunity to show the earth its brilliancy. I was alone, and, save the splash of my paddle and the occasional unearthly call of the loon, all was still as the grave. In entering a narrow passage to avoid the weeds, I had to hug the land so close that occasionally the limb of a tree would brush against me or my birch-bark canoe. With a suddenness that made my heart's blood run cold, a yell from some unknown beast, loud, shrill, and unearthly, so close that I almost believed for a moment that the cause was within reach, echoed from tree to tree, and died away, reverberating in the distance. Again and again it was repeated. For awhile I remained motionless, till the cool breeze recalled me to myself, and I proceeded homewards. Next morning I returned to examine the place. A veteran hunter was my companion, and we found such convincing proofs that bears had been there, that one of them I feel certain produced this noise, my companion assuring me that at the period the sexes come together, if rivals are in the way, the call or note of defiance is quite dissimilar from their general voice.

Early in spring the young are born. At first they are very small. In six weeks they are able to accompany their mother, who cares for them with the greatest solicitude and attention, hauling the logs on one side for the cubs to obtain the coveted grubs and larvæ underneath; pulling down the uppermost branches that produce fruit; and if, by accident, the young should be placed in a position of danger, her life is always willingly sacrificed in their defence.

Walking across a portage in Maine, close to the borders of New Brunswick, in front of the party of which I was a member, my gun loaded, in the hope of killing a partridge or two, I perceived a small animal, about the size of a King Charles spaniel, running along the track a hundred or more yards in front of me. Without troubling myself to look closely, I concluded it was a porcupine, animals which were extremely common in the vicinity. Soon after a dog belonging to one of my companions passed me; stooping to the trail he gave tongue, and went in pursuit at his best possible speed. In a few more moments I knew he had brought something to bay, and, proceeding to his assistance, I found a young bear, the size of a badger, treed in a six-inch sapling. Where was the mother? Answer says, "Don't know;" for young Bruin, after a vixenish fight, was secured, and, although half-an-hour elapsed in the operation, the old lady still remained *non est*.

It is very common for bears to be killed after they have retired to their dormitory for the winter sleep. When living near Lake Couchachin, in Canada, I assisted on such an occasion. An Indian from Rama came to me in great haste, with the hope I would sell him some ammunition. From his earnestness and anxiety I knew that he had made a valuable discovery, which, after a little higgling, was disclosed. He had found a bear's retreat in a hollow log, nearly imbedded in snow, and the ammunition was for poor Bruin's destruction.

Stipulating that I should have a share of the sport, I supplied the ammunition, and we started. The distance was short. Mr. Chippewa Indian knocked on the log, and the writer stood at the entrance. Poor Bruin at length forsook his snug retreat, yawning and looking stupid as he emerged into daylight, when a bullet at less than five yards settled the matter. When a bear is thus housed in a log a heavy vapour of steam, should the weather be calm, perceptibly hangs over it.

Many naturalists for years considered this species

identical with the bear of Europe; but of later date all those accepted as authorities have agreed that the black bear of America and the bear of Europe are totally distinct species; and if any of my readers should have the opportunity, let them closely examine both, which will be found together at the Regent's Park Gardens, in London, and they will no longer hesitate that the conclusion is the correct one.

CHAPTER XII.

FLIGHT SHOOTING ON GRAND PRAIRIE.

WHILE resting for a day or two at MacComb's, Grand Prairie, Illinois, when on a tour, at the commencement of severe weather, one of the hands who had been out collecting cattle on the prairie, on returning to dinner, informed me that both ducks and geese were arriving in immense numbers. Soon my No. 10 gun was brought out, and with seven pounds of shot and my large powder-flask full, I started in the direction indicated. The weather since morning had undergone a complete change, for instead of a damp, mild atmosphere, snow was falling in large but few flakes, with the thermometer below freezing-point.

On reaching the sloughs I found birds abundant, but too wary for great success; so, after firing a few long shots with indifferent success, I determined to change my beat. I had remarked the day before a field of a few acres of indifferent Indian corn which had not yet been gathered, and which was excessively wet and soft from the dampness of the soil; thither I determined to turn my footsteps, and well it was I did so, for a finer afternoon's sport I have seldom enjoyed. Before I got within a quarter of a mile of my destination, I could see duck in numerous large flights hovering over the place in question, giving hopes of sharp work. On gaining the edge of the field and taking a survey, I found the ground in many places perfectly covered with birds, and strings of fresh arrivals coming in momentarily—mallard, butter duck, teal and winter duck, all making the best use of their bills to further destroy an indifferent crop. After a survey of the situation I selected a stand, forming a screen of corn stems and iron weed, and scarcely was I ensconced, when the honk! bonk! honk! of a distant flock of wild geese told me that the wary scoundrels were *en avant*. However, so many duck came within easy shooting distance that I could not resist opening fire, and I commenced skirmishing forthwith. The birds appeared totally devoid of fear either of the report of my gun or my presence, and flew frequently within fifteen or twenty yards in the most leisurely and business-like manner. Again and again I loaded and shot till my barrels got agreeably warm. Old Nep, whom doubtless many companions remember, soon had the ground around my feet thickly strewn with slain, and when an unfortunate duck less severely peppered than others, or only broken-winged, would attempt to hobble off, Master Nep would give him a pinch about the regions of the cranium that immediately reduced the most obstreperous to submission. Geese commenced to arrive after I had been at work about half an hour; first a solitary gander, whose coat I dusted and secured, next two or three, and ultimately half-dozens and dozens in squads, while the duck whistled by with all the velocity of sky-rockets. By four P.M. my powder-flask commenced to show signs of giving out, and with sickly, hollow rattle proclaimed that the remaining charges were few. To prolong the sport I reduced my charges, but still the end was drawing near and could only be delayed a few minutes, for with regret, though the snow was now falling fast and the weather anything but enjoyable, I was brought to a halt. On collecting the spoil I had nineteen geese and forty-one ducks, a load sufficient for a Canadian pony. However, I managed to stow them all in a fence corner, there to remain till sent for, and most unwillingly I turned towards home. My last view of the field was of broad bills in even increasing regiments rushing on to the devoted crop, and I have little doubt if my ammunition had lasted that I could have shown a score that had seldom previously been made.

The society of a companion was the only thing wanting to complete the enjoyment; for talking over the results by a comfortable fire, with a goodly supply of tobacco and a hot glass of Scotch whiskey punch, is no small portion of the pleasure of the day's amusement and a fitting climax. Moreover, such exploits are a bond of fellowship with a comrade which does more to promote good feeling than aught else I know of. If one of my old friends had been with me, that duck hunt would have doubtlessly formed a standing dish at our most frequented haunt for the greater part of the winter, or till some performance more brilliant had taken place, to throw the old yarn in the shade and eclipse its splendour.

CHAPTER XIII.

SALMON FISHING IN LABRADOR.

HALIFAX,—reader, have you ever been in Halifax? Many places are to be found less to be admired and less agreeable to live in, although I have heard sailors quote the saying, usually applied to its namesake in Old England, "deliver us from Hell, Hull, and Halifax." Why this condemnation, I know not. For my part, I have been in many towns less pleasant; the inhabitants are hospitable and genial, the society is good, and the ladies have no small pretensions to being considered beautiful. Having spent a couple of weeks lounging about Halifax with nothing to do, at length I decided to go in search of adventure, and, if possible, get a few days' salmon fishing.

Having come to this conclusion, on examining the local papers, I found that the good schooner *Alert*, registered A 1, would sail on the morrow for the Straits of Belle Isle, to collect salt fish from the coast, weather permitting, so without delay I hastened to the designated wharf, to examine the craft, and strike a bargain with the skipper. The captain was below, in the cabin, one of the deck hands informed me, as I passed the gangway, indicating the position of the companion-ladder with a jerk of his finger over the left shoulder. On getting at the bottom of that most inconvenient piece of mechanism in every small craft, the companion-ladder,—a little faster than expected, having slipped my foot on the second or third step, and slid the rest of the way to the bottom, only saving my neck by the hold I had of the banisters, and making a tremendous racket by my rapid descent,—I was saluted with, "Jock, you careless lubber, can't you mind your feet? This is the second time you have made that infernal clatter this day!" And what more would have come I know not, for I interrupted the speaker in his invective by knocking with considerable energy at the door, which appeared to stand between us. On being desired to enter, I turned the handle, when Captain MacGregor was presented to my view, lathered all over, and in the act of giving the finishing touch on the strap to his razor. He was a big man, powerful, raw-boned, but kindly-looking, and with great courtesy he apologised for his undress, and the rough salute he had given me; the companion-ladder he condemned in no measured terms, but at the same time he could make no allowance for a young callan like Jock being not spry enough with his feet to keep a grip of aucht that he could get his heel or toe on. I saw that the skipper was a bit of a character, and with all his external roughness, had a good, warm, kind heart underneath. I determined, therefore, to trust myself to his seamanship, if suitable terms could be made. At once the subject of my visit was broached and his charge for the trip ascertained. After thinking a minute or two, he asked my name, and whether or no I was from the States. On being answered in the negative and my cognomen given, he took a good look at me, and laying down his razor, the lather being still on his face, he delivered himself in these words :—" The passage I'll just charge you five pund sterling for. I'm thinking you'll na deem that ower muckle, but if I didna like your cut, twenty pund, let alone five, would na hae let you aboard. And I suppose it's a' right, and gin you'll jist wait till I get scraped, I can gie you a glass of real Islay that nare was gauged by exciseman." Soon the scraping operation was performed to his satisfaction, and a black bottle was produced the contents of which fully reached the proper standard of excellence, if strength is considered to constitute it. In the meantime the captain had got ready to go on shore, and Jock was summoned for final instructions, but the deck hands stated that he was not on board, but fishing off the end of the dock. A stentorian shout summoned the truant. With line in hand and a string of flounders he made his appearance. "How darst you gang ashore wi'out my permission. You're mair bother than the whole ship's company, you de'il's buckey you. Yinst we get hame, your mither maun keep you to hersel, for though she be my ain sister, I'll no be longer fashed wi' the likes o' you. Now listen to me: hae dinner sharp at twa; see that the cook dun'na boil the haggis ower muckle, and set twa places. You'll tak your dinner wi' me, sir; I ha got a real Scotch haggis, and the likes you maybe nare tasted afore. I'll tak no refusal, mon, unless you're promised to a friend." With pleasure I accepted the invitation, and, much pleased with both captain and schooner, returned to the hotel to pack my traps and make final arrangements before sailing. Sharp at two I was again on board, and the agreeable odour which pervaded the craft, if it rose from the haggis, was a guarantee of future excellence. The captain welcomed me with great warmth, and expressed hopes that we should have a rapid and pleasant passage, but at the same time informed me that there was no more kittlish navigation in the world, excepting it be on his own native coast. Our meal passed pleasantly, and while performing the office of host, his brusqueness disappeared, and with it a good deal of the broad dialect. The haggis was excellent, the bacon and chickens were as good, and the West Indian preserves which formed the dessert were of the best quality. As I stretched my limbs under his table, in the snug little cabin, after the cloth had been removed, and a kettle of boiling water flanked with lemons had made its appearance, I felt satisfied that there were worse lots in the world than commanding a clipper schooner in the West Indian trade.

As the toddy circulated our companionship increased, and to a question I asked in reference to his success in the last voyage, he made the following statement:—"Well, sir, you see a man that commenced the world without a bawbee. My father and mither were baith poor, and when I thought I had enough schooling, our family being big, I bound myself as an apprentice on board a bark called the *Kilmore*, that traded out of Clyde to the West Indies. She was one of the old-fashioned sort, and would make as much on a wind as a hay-stack. Still, she was a snug little boat, strong as oak and dry as could be. On the last run I made in her the captain took sick and died, most before we lost sight of Cantire. This made me second mate, and the former first mate took charge. Our voyage was prosperous, and we dropped anchor off Demerara in near the shortest time that then ever had been made. One thing only disturbed the harmony of the passage, viz., the acting first officer was so puffed up with his new post that he neither performed his duty or would let others do theirs. The temporary captain was, after a deal of forbearance, compelled to place him under arrest, and prefer charges against him on dropping anchor. The result was, he was discharged, and as the bark was to go to sea immediately, and a first mate could not be procured, I was advanced to act in that capacity.

"When we got back to Clyde, the very day we sighted old Ailsa Craig, my time was out, and as we ran up the river with a fair wind astern, and all our stunsails set, I would have given most aught if my mither and father—who lived at Saltcoats, close by—could have seen their boy, in his new and advanced berth. The owners of the old *Kilmore* launched a new ship next year, and, much to my unexpected satisfaction, I got the berth of first officer in her. A year or two after, when at Jamaica, I was offered the command of a brig in the Honduras trade, and here I saved some money; in three years I purchased a share, and in two years more was half owner. The world prospered wi' me, and every few year or so I see the auld folks and gie them a little comfort in their auld age. When young, many's the trout I had tane, and when I would make my fleeing visits to the old hearthstone, I would generally get a day or two to try the salmon in Doon, for I was aye fond o' fishing, so was my father, and his father afore him, an' somehow I ne'er kent a fisher who was na an honest man "—(as he warmed with the subject he resumed his native dialect),—" and when I looked at you, and heard you say you were going for a bit o' fishing, my heart warmed to you, and tho' I ha' been so fashed wi' passengers, and had maist made up my mind nare to take anither, I jist thought I'd brak my rule on your account."

The afternoon passed pleasantly; the captain had been everywhere, and discoursed with great good sense and knowledge upon different countries, and he was destitute of the disagreeable egotism that so frequently stamps our uneducated countrymen. Moreover, he was a loyal and true subject of his queen and country, which made me the more appreciate him. Next morning we got to sea with a fair wind, and every prospect of a short run; the schooner was a remarkably fast sailer, built after the model of one of our modern yachts, low and close to the water; with plenty of beam, and long, tapering, rakish spars. Her decks were without hamper, and showed from their whiteness that holystone was not spared; while the crew, which consisted of six men, the redoubtable Jock, and a sturdy nigger, were as efficient, clean, and smart as could well have been found. The captain took a great deal of pleasure in his craft, and handled her as none but a man of experience could; besides, he was half owner, and this made him have an ·interest in all the details that one employed by the month or cruise would be unlikely to possess. In talking to the skipper, reading, and looking over my tackle, the day passed rapidly, and as night closed in and the breeze lessened, I concluded that I had seldom passed a pleasanter day.

After supper, MacGregor produced his rods and fly book for my inspection, and a long and careful examination we had of these common subjects of interest. His rods were remarkably heavy, longer than I should deem necessary, while his flies were coarsely tied, although the colouring was all that could be desired. If one had been dismembered, I have little doubt, from the dubbing and feathers of which it was composed, three, or at least two, of my treasures could have been fabricated. Of course, I soon produced my tools, to all of which he gave an abundance of praise, but doubted if they could do more execution than his own. My reel, alone, he acknowledged to be better than his, and concluded, if ever he went to New York,* he'd be guilty of the extravagance of purchasing its counterpart. Bedtime arrived, and having discussed a night cap, I turned into my bunk, while the captain went on deck to keep the middle watch with the second mate—a practice he always followed when on the coast. The motion was just sufficient to lull me to sleep, and soon my eyes were closed to the outer world. Three hours at the utmost must I have been asleep, when the violence of the motion, the stamping on deck, and the stentorian voice of the skipper, thoroughly aroused me from my slumbers. From the even keel that we had been on a few hours before, we now careened so far over that I found it next to impossible to brace myself in my berth; the wind fairly screeched through the rigging, and the racket caused by chairs, and other movables adrift, banished slumber for the time being. At length I could remain no longer below, from a desire to see and ascertain the nature of our position. After many ineffectual attempts, and not without assuming all kinds of strange attitudes, I got into my nether garments and boots, and succeeded in gaining the upper regions. The scene was truly terrific; the sea was wild with agitation; billow after billow rolled past, crested with foam, while the blast fairly howled

* Made by Andrew Clerk and Co., of Maiden Lane.

about us. The captain stood aft, holding on to the weather mainstay, occasionally giving an order to the men at the wheel. From the spread of canvas we had formerly carried we were now reduced to a close-reefed mainsail, foresail, and storm jib. Sometimes the vessel would appear to jump, as she would leave the top of one roller to reach the next. Nobly the gallant craft bore the ordeal, and splendidly did she behave; still, the cool self-possession of the captain failed to prevent my thinking how much better I should be satisfied to be again standing on *terra firma*, and although pride prevented my making the confession, I internally registered a vow, that if ever I again placed my foot on land, nothing should again tempt me to trust my safety on board a coaster.

I fear, however, my vow had no more stability in it than many made by others under similar circumstances. On the coast of China I was on board a vessel which had the misfortune to be caught in a typhoon, and all thought our last hour was not far distant. The person who commanded her was the most profane man it ever was my chance to encounter; he could not give an order of the most simple nature without qualifying it with an oath. As sea after sea broke over us, and we were in momentary danger of being swamped, I heard him say that if he got out of this fix he'd never use a foul word again. The vortex of the storm soon afterwards passed to leeward, and we were safe; but this swearer changed not from his evil habit, but, if anything, swore more. On another occasion, proceeding from Malta to Naples, I encountered a gregali or levanter—a violent description of storm frequent in that portion of the globe. The vessel I had shipped in was a small brig, of Trieste, manned by Albanians, Greeks, and Italians. As soon as our position became one of danger, all appeared paralysed and incapable, through fear, of performing the slightest duties. In the after part of the brig a niche was fitted up with some pictures of the Virgin, and various saints, with two or three candlesticks, the whole intended to represent a chapel; around this the mongrel crew crowded, praying and counting their beads. One who appeared more devout or terrified than the rest, and whom I had previously remarked from his villainous cast of countenance, kept promising in all the most impressive language he could select, silver candlesticks, and other expensive ornaments to the shrine of his patron saint, if he would only interpose to save him this time. Three days after we dropped anchor in the Bay of Bays. Giovanni's vows and promises had stirred my curiosity, as I was certain his meagre pay would not fulfil one-half of what he doubtlessly had intended. Wandering a few days afterwards in one of the loneliest suburbs, I came across my quondam acquaintance, in the middle of a number of lazzaroni, engaged in gambling. The scene tempted me to remain and see the sequel, which was not far off, for after fifteen minutes he arose, shook himself, pronounced an anathema on his luck, and disappeared. Having to visit the brig, in reference to some baggage I had left on board, I found Giovanni on deck, when I asked him if he had provided the offerings he had promised his saint. With a jocular smile he acknowledged he had not, but intended doing it at some future, indefinite date. I fear human nature is much the same everywhere, under whatever clime, or in whatever land it may be nurtured. Mussulman, Roman Catholic, or Protestant—all make promises or vows on the spur or compulsion of the moment, too often afterwards, under happier auspices, to be disregarded.

But to my narrative. With each hour the gale increased, and to such violence that the gallant schooner was momentarily in peril. Next morning dawned bleak and wild, the waves tumbled over one another, the larger swallowing up the lesser for want of something else to satisfy their devouring inclination. This day and several others were only a repetition of the first night; no reckoning could be obtained; still we stood upon our course. With half an eye I could detect that our skipper was uneasy, and anxious again for a glimpse of the old familiar sun.

One of our sails had been blown to ribbons, and our bowsprit became partially sprung, still as long as we had plenty of sea-room all was comparatively safe; sailors' ingenuity had obviated temporarily the injury of the latter, and the sail room had supplied fresh canvas. The fourth evening the gale exhausted itself about midnight, and I, who had not closed an eye during these days, experienced a few hours of the balmiest sleep that ever fell to the lot of storm-tossed mariner, notwithstanding that there was not a dry stitch, even among the bedding, on board the *Alert*. How often do I think of the affectionate, kind mother of my childhood, and her anxiety that her boy should not sleep in damp sheets! Could she see or know the trials and hardships which he, with others, has encountered in his journey through life, her maternal solicitude would receive a severe shock. Truly, the journey of life is a rough path, made up of storms and sunshine, wintry snows and tropical showers; one time ascending hills, the next descending; fortune smiling to-day, frowning to-morrow; ignorant of what the future has in store for us; but, doubtless, all is for the best, and those troubles and temptations which in our spleen we grumble at, are but intended to fit us for our ultimate resting-place, where perpetual sunshine and unclouded happiness will reign for ever.

Next morning when day awoke me, I was delighted to find that we were once more on a level keel, and when I gained the deck, so bright and joyous appeared the weather, that you could imagine that nature was laughing and enjoying our previous discomfort. Sambo, the cook, soon supplied me with a cup of coffee, which, with my morning pipe, I thoroughly enjoyed, while I watched the detached banks of fog roll lazily over the water, occasionally shutting out or opening vistas of the distance. The whole water was alive with fish, the surface in many places being broken, and resembling the rapids of a river, with their gambols, but soon a giant porpoise would roll in among them, when all the terrified fry would disappear for a few minutes, to re-present themselves when the intruder had departed. Gulls, in immense numbers, floated upon the water, as if resting from the fatigue caused by the war of the elements, and adding beauty to the picture by their pure white, spotless plumage. I remember hearing an old salt in answer to the question of why sea fowl, in bad weather, so much more fearlessly approach vessels than when it is calm, give the following solution :—" Well, you see, those good folks who die don't go to Davie Jones, but turn into cape pigeons and kittiwakes, and them kind of birds, and when they think it's rough and kind of dangerous, they naturally like to hover about their friends to protect them." If angels visit earth in these modern and wicked times, there are many garbs they could assume less beautiful and less suitable than that of the snowy-white sea-gull.

At breakfast our captain expressed much satisfaction at the bad weather having passed, and particularly at its being so unusually calm, for he much feared, what with the usual incorrectness of dead reckoning and strong tides—which exist to a greater extent here * than probably in any other portion of the globe— that he was some way off his course. On taking soundings, the depth indicated by the lead line and the composition of the bottom so completely differed from what we expected that there scarcely remained a doubt that we were astray; still we were drifting very rapidly to the north-west, the fog, if anything, growing denser. About eleven our captain, having given the look-out strict injunctions to keep his eyes open while he again went below to examine his chart, I followed suit. I could scarcely have been in the cabin over five minutes when the schooner received a severe shock, which caused me to rush on

* In the Bay of Fundy the tide sometimes rises over twenty feet.

deck. We had struck a rock forward, a little to starboard of the stem, but the tide had fortunately swung us round clear, and we were drifting on as if nothing had happened. On sounding, we found we were making water rapidly, faster than the pumps could throw it out. True, we had the boats, and our danger was trifling, but the security of the gallant craft was imminent. Not a word of anger did the captain permit to escape his lips, but accepted all as destiny. Scarcely twenty minutes had we been in this uncertain state when a gentle breeze sprang up and the fog rapidly lifted, giving us an observation, and disclosing a panorama never to be forgotten. Tier after tier of sterile hills overtopped each other to the north, grand in their bold and fantastic outline, while a white sandy beach met the blue water, occasionally interrupted by a reef of rocks jutting out into the azure element. Not over a mile separated us from the shore, and projecting headlands shut us in from west and easterly gales; while a reef of rocks, the extremity of which we had touched, formed a natural breakwater a mile and a half to the eastward. If so disposed, with the wind from its present direction, we should have found it a difficult matter to beat out, and when the skipper informed me that he intended running in and stranding the vessel at the first high tide, I not only highly approved, but was much delighted with the prospect. The welcome word to let go the anchor soon rang forth, and the emblem of faith took hold on firm sand at four fathoms.

In discussing our early dinner, the captain informed me that he intended going ashore to seek out a suitable place to strand his craft, and that I might as well accompany him and explore to the westward, for a stream was marked on his chart which could not be over a few miles from our anchorage. Soon we trod terra firma, and, while MacGregor remained, I started, double-barrel in hand, on a reconnaissance, with light steps and lighter heart. The soil was thin and unproductive, bearing nothing but stunted brush, excepting in the ravines and hollows, sheltered from the prevailing winds; here a dwarf deformed pine or stunted larch would rear its diminutive head, or an antiquated birch, covered with its hoary bark, hang precarious from a jutting rock. Intense solitude reigned around, and nought broke the stillness of the landscape, save the persevering, wicked hum of the bloodthirsty mosquito. With buoyant hopes I walked on, and just as I began to think I had traversed quite two miles, I suddenly came upon the margin of a bright, pure river, about seventy yards wide, running in a continuous, rapid stream towards the sea. Mungo Park's first view of the Niger, or Speke and Grant's first sight of the upper waters of the Nile, can scarce have afforded more satisfaction to those illustrious travellers than I experienced on this occasion. Several seals were fishing in the current, and their disregard of my presence convinced me that their acquaintance with the lords of creation had been very limited. Several families of wild duck were conspicuous, while salmon and sea trout broke water wherever the stream was undisturbed by the unwelcome seals. Reader, have you ever been on rivers and witnessed how rapidly the arrival of a seal in a pool is transmitted? The moment before his unwelcome presence is known, thousands of fish sport themselves, but on his advent being published, not an indication can be noted that aught else tenants the water save this amphibious animal. After taking a due survey I started upwards, following the margin of the stream. In less than a mile I found its general characteristics changed, and from a steady rapid current it became a boiling, seething cataract. Again its character changed, and large sombre-looking pools interrupted its precipitous course. How I longed for a rod! It required much less experience than mine to be aware that this was a magnificent fishing-ground. Salmon rose on all sides, pitching themselves clear of the water and making it fly in spray, like the splash of a heavy stone. I had beheld enough to satisfy the most fastidious, and with hurried steps I retraced my way, brimful with what I had seen, and anxious to convey the important information to my kind and worthy acquaintance, the captain.

That evening we discussed our plans, MacGregor being in excellent spirits, having found that the ship's leak could easily be stopped, and that the injury was far from serious. As he was his own employer, he thought he would indulge in a little recreation, and set his men to painting, sail-making, and all those minor *et ceteras* so constantly wanted on board ship, while we in company flogged the river, or otherwise enjoyed ourselves. That night we sat up later than usual, and fishing excursions for years gone by were discussed, tales told of the first blood we had drawn, of the largest fish we had captured, and where they had succumbed to our prowess. Old, musty, moth-eaten fly-hooks and feathers, that appeared as if they had not not seen the light of day for years, were produced from his numerous lockers, and as they were examined, and various pages turned over, numerous were the anecdotes narrated in connection with each. So the evening sped along, and chancing to refer to the sea-trout, he seized upon the subject as on a favourite hobby, and informed me that "if there were whitling,* he would show me some sport ere we reached the river, for he kent of a flie that they could na resist ava, but just loupet at it like mad." His fly-hooks were again appealed to, but a perfect specimen could not be found; some wanted wings, others bodies, and in all the gut was in an imperfect state. What was to be done? As luck would have it, I fortunately had the materials, and his *débris* afforded a good pattern. On offering them for his use, he declined, but requested me to become manufacturer. The fly was simple, and easily tied; and for the benefit of those who may some day be similarly situated, I will here describe it. Wings from the swan or white goose; body scarlet mohair; two or three strands of scarlet ibis for the tail; the body wrapped loosely and wide with silver tinsel, with a scarlet hackle under the wings. In half-an-hour I had tied six; and taking a night-cap in the shape of a strong glass of the genuine Islay in the form of punch, turned in to dream of fish and fishing.

Jock roused us an hour before daylight, and having discussed an excellent cup of coffee, we got into the stern sheets of one of the boats, with two of the crew to pull us to our destination. After leaving the side of the schooner, MacGregor determined to

* Scotticism for sea-trout.

mount one of the flies which I had made the previous evening, and troll behind the boat. Soon the deception was overboard, and scarcely had twenty yards left the reel before he had a strike, but the fish did not hold. On satisfying himself that the tackle had not parted, more line was paid out, and ere we had progressed a hundred yards, he hooked a fish, and that a good one. The reel rushed with the greatest velocity, although the rowers had backed water to impede the progress of the boat, and for a good quarter of an hour it was give and take. The scientific manner in which my friend handled his rod at once convinced me that he was no novice, and his coolness proved that he was master of the art. At length the previously unseen and game antagonist was brought under the gunwale, and with little difficulty I struck the gaff into his beautiful side, and brought him into the boat. My friend called the captured fish a pollack, and confessed to having killed hundreds of them on his native coast. I have since become aware that he was right, and that this fish is well known in British waters. Again his flies were astern, and similar results took place, till I got impatient lest we should be late in arriving at our destination. So far we had not seen a sea-trout, but this delay was not to be long continued. On entering the estuary of the river, our first one was hooked—a lively fellow of three pounds; another and another followed suit, till over a dozen white struggling beauties lay upon the foot-boards. I am convinced, if we had remained and devoted ourselves to this sport, that we could almost, between the two rods, have loaded the boat; but nobler game was in prospect, and splendid fishing was resigned for sport in prospective.

Before leaving the white trout, a few words on its habits and characteristics may not be inappropriate. Along the coast of Labrador and Prince Edward's Island, about the mouth of the numerous rivers that flow into the St. Lawrence, they are to be found in immense numbers, visiting the various streams about the time, or perhaps a little later, than the salmon. Their size varies from one-and-a-half to six pounds, or even more. They spawn in fresh water, like salmon, which they much resemble in shape and habit. They are greedy feeders, easily hooked, and not fastidious in their taste; and, for their weight, are second to no fish in the world for their persevering, determined efforts to escape, jumping frequently several feet clear of the water, and using every effort to tax the angler's skill.

In appearance the sea-trout* is much like the *Salmo salar*, and when cooked it would be difficult to tell the two apart. In fishing for them, the same skill in the

* The sea trout of America and Britain are different species.

choice of flies is not necessary, but brilliant ones should always be selected, for invariably they will be found the most effective. If in a boat, the angler should generally confine himself to such portions of the coast as receive the fresh water of a river or brook. The flies that I should prefer using for this description of sport would be at least several sizes smaller than those commonly employed for the capture of the larger species (*Salmo salar*).

Having pulled up into the current as far as the stream would permit, we landed upon a rock, behind whose jutting sides the water formed many a miniature whirlpool. As the captain raised his rod to take in the surplus line, a fine sea-trout rose at the fly. Judging from the splash, he was of more than usual size, and worth making a second effort for. Again the cunningly-disguised hook was passed over his retreat, but with the same success; a third trial was essayed, and as the third time is said to be lucky, so it proved, for the fish was hooked. The struggles and devices this fish practised to escape were worthy of success; three times he ran out many a yard of line, and on each occasion jumped several times clear of the water; but all was futile, for after upwards of ten minutes' play, he was obliged to surrender to skill and practice. My companion called upon me to use the gaff, and with the first effort I succeeded in landing him on terra firma. We had no scales to weigh him, and we were too tired, and had killed nobler specimens before we returned to think more of this little hero; but from experience I am confident he must have reached nearly five pounds. On examination of our ground, we mutually agreed to separate, one taking the left, and the other the right side of the river. Trees and brush did not grow sufficiently near its margin to seriously incommode us, and the rocks, which became uninterrupted after leaving the coast, were flat and in regular strata, affording excellent footing, and in many places their table-like surface was only a few inches above the level of the stream. One of the sailors accompanied me to act as gaffer, and afford assistance, while the other went with the captain. In our council of war, which we held before separating, it was determined that we should try and fish opposite one another as much as circumstances would allow, and under no occasion get out of hail. A few hundred yards higher than my exploring had led me the day before, the water tumbled over some rocks, making a fall of six or seven feet, and then expanded into a broad sullen pool, with a disturbed but slow current down its centre, covered with patches of foam. Soon my rod was together, and an old favourite fly added to my stretcher, whose performance was frequently on previous occasions satisfactory. This fly has no name that I am aware of; in fact, I go so far as to imagine myself the inventor; but whether my title is good or not to this honour, I will give its description, *pro bono publico*. Wings from the wing feathers of the bustard (a bird now to be found in quantity only on the steppes of southern Russia or Tartary: in plumage and colour it much resembles the wild turkey, whose feathers, I have no doubt, would answer equally well), with a few strands of the scarlet macaw or ibis mixed with it. Body of two colours, equally divided; upper portion of dark blue mohair, lower of gingery red, a red hackle round the lower portions of body, and a black round the upper. A band of silver tinsel, if for a bright day, and gold, if for a dark one, wrapped carefully and regularly between the hackles; the whole terminating with a scarlet tail either of ibis or worsted, —the latter I prefer. To say that this fly has not been tried previously might be deemed presumptuous; but this I will say, that when I first made it, I had no pattern, neither did I try to copy anything I had seen. I have used it in many waters, and invariably with success, although I am aware that frequently what is found most deadly on some streams is totally ineffective in a neighbouring river.

My fly being on, and the cast well stretched, I commenced operations, and at the third throw rose a heavy fish without pricking him. However, I thought I would move down, and return when I had got to the bottom of the pool, and offer his excellency another chance. At the fifth throw I rose and hooked a fine fish, who, as soon as he felt he was impaled, rushed down into the still water. Not less than seventy yards did he run out at this burst, and when I thought I had turned him, the scoundrel sulked and remained sullen at the bottom. I thought he was hooked strong, for I struck him quick and forcibly, and therefore felt confident, barring accidents, that he was destined to be mine. Slowly, but surely, I worked down stream, taking in with guarded hand every inch of slack that I could with safety. When abreast of him, not over thirty yards were off my reel, and the ground was more than usually accessible. With patience I waited some minutes, but I might just as well have been fast to a rock. Other salmon were breaking around me, and I could not afford the time to remain inactive. I was determined to rouse my prize, and my anxiety increased when the sailor who accompanied me announced that the skipper had just landed a fish. In my excitement I had lost sight of my friend, but Crosby's news recalled him. The captain had drawn first blood. This fact brought my impatience to boiling-point, and I could stand it no longer. Crosby was instructed to throw a few stones above the fish, and thus endeavour to start him from his retreat. The first piece of rock had scarcely touched the water when the object was attained. Off he went, with the velocity of electricity, and the handle of my reel spun round like the fly-wheel of an engine; although I kept a considerable check upon my line, still over ninety yards must have run off, when, much to my satisfaction, he broke water three times, the first time throwing himself good three feet clear of his element. This manœuvre, although frequently successful, pleased me in one way. I was certain that his route would now be changed, and probably I should succeed in getting in some of my line. True to my former experience, the fish now headed up stream, and permitted himself to be somewhat controlled. At moderate pace he retraced his steps, and almost had got to where I struck him, when, putting a little more strain on than he admired, round he wheeled, and with his previous velocity pointed his head again for the sea. Still, the struggle had its effect; this dash was not equal to previous ones, and fifty yards of line brought him up. For ten minutes it was give and take, back and forward, up and down, till at last I brought him, all resplendent in his silvery armour, into shoal water. "Now, Crosby, now's your chance; careful, man; don't be in too big a hurry." But my advice was disregarded; the sailor made a plunge at the fish with the gaff as if it had been a harpoon, scratched the salmon's side, and all my work was again before me. The drawing of blood instilled new vitality into the fish's veins, and the previously beaten, vanquished foe was running out line as if he had been fresh struck. I could not be angry; when a novice I had done likewise, and, no doubt, my attendant had just made his virgin effort. In fact, I could not help being amused at his astonished countenance, for, doubtless, he had already counted the fish as safe. This last struggle did not continue long; again I got him in shoal water, when, having cautioned and instructed my excited attendant as far as words could avail, he made a second effort, and that correctly. Twelve pounds was the weight of this noble salmon, and often have I found that those of this size are more game and afford a harder fight than larger fish. The strain on your rod is not so severe, or the contest so long as with a heavier antagonist, but the activity and energy displayed are sharper.

Having overhauled my tackle, and lit a weed as a reward for my prowess, I again ascended to the top of the pool and commenced afresh; visions of the first fish

I rose, which I felt convinced was a formidable one, inducing me to this course. My leader had now got straightened, from the action of the water, and the strain it had so lately successfully withstood. To get my line clear away to the requisite length, I threw across the surging portion of the stream and dipped my tip, to prevent any unnecessary delay when I reached my friend's ambush; a couple of casts brought me to the spot, and with careful, steady hand and measured throw I placed my fly, straight as a bee line,* a few yards above where my prey was supposed to be lodged; and with that regular motion that resembles the passage of a shrimp through the water, I brought the bright, fascinating deception towards me, the current at the same time carrying it downwards. Description, particularly if you enter into detail, is always longer than action. My handsome imitation—of what? for a similar living fly I never saw—was a foot or two above the desired eddy, when a splash, a flourish of a broad, dark tail, answered by my quick, nervous hand giving an electric strike, fastened me to a splendid fish. As man and animals choose different methods of assault or defence, so this salmon chose a different course to free himself. The hook had scarcely been in him,

* A common Americanism, originating from loaded bees always flying straight to their home.

when four times he sprang with determined energy from his watery home, each spring causing me, in courtesy, to lower the point of my weapon, as an inferior would salute a senior officer; but this steeple-chase escapade had not the desired effect, and the salmon, comprehending this, altered his plan of combat, and settled down deep in the pellucid river, remaining immovable and inactive, although far from conquered. An occasion of this kind is a trying ordeal, and often as dangerous to the tackle as any stratagem that is put in practice; in fact, I have thought that it is practised for the purpose of rubbing their snout on the rocks or gravel, as frequently I have found, after killing a fish who had thus performed, that my fly was much frayed and worn.

After waiting for many minutes, trusting that my foe would change his mind and his quarters, I became impatient, and believing my tackle to be good, put on a little extra purchase; this *ruse* was successful, for with astounding velocity the fish started down stream, at racing pace, for parts unknown. The reel fairly yelled, and instead of the well-made sonorous click being heard, a discordant screech was its utterance. Close on a hundred yards of line rushed through the heated rings before he slackened up, and a good twenty yards more I had followed his course; at the end of this dash he broke water splendidly, causing the spray to fly for many feet around. Again and again his argentine flanks reflected brilliant radii in the sunlight, and at each glistening reflection of the solar rays I feared that we should part company without the most remote chance of further or more closely renewing our acquaintance. Fortune and good tackle, however, favoured me; and I had the satisfaction of turning his head for the source of the river, and probable birthplace of himself and relations. With the greatest satisfaction I took in yard after yard, my hopes rising as the body of my reel expanded; at length I saw the loop which attached the line to the leader, and the sight caused me more satisfaction than one can possibly imagine who is daily engaged in the ordinary pursuits of life. O salmon fishing! what pleasure have I enjoyed following thy peaceful pursuit! What ecstasy, what delight! Would that I had the pen of the most fluent writer, or tongue of the most eloquent spokesman! I could do you far more justice; but still I doubt if it is in the power of words to mete to you an iota of the laudation and praise your fascinations so eminently deserve.

Why wander from facts? Simply because I cannot help it. But if I must be recalled from the enchantment of scenes which may never be re-acted, bear with me for a moment; it is but the allotted time for a breather between the heats—the welcome respite before the final burst that is to terminate the race. So it was in this instance; the strength, if not the courage of the regal foe, was weaker, and each succeeding effort became less powerful. Many a yard of line was again run out and safely restored to its resting-place. Up and down both immolator and victim traced and retraced their course; the one fearing to pursue, the other momentarily becoming more unfit. Time did its work, and, as in all things, brought the last scene to a close. A shoal bank of gravel lay at my feet, and giving my fish the butt, I drew him in towards Crosby, who, ankle deep, stood beneath me in the cool, clear water, and struck the gaff into the spotless silver side, and landed him with the adroitness of one who had served a long apprenticeship to the trade. Don't imagine that there is no science in handling a gaff; for one expert many muffs will be found. How, then, you may ask, did this sailor learn so difficult a business in so short a space? Probably because he had a natural aptness; or, more likely, being a sailor, he could turn his hands much sooner than persons of any other trade to a business which required coolness and dexterity.

This fish weighed over eighteen pounds, and was

fresh run from the sea, for he had not yet cleansed himself of the sea-lice; his breadth and depth were enormous in proportion to his length—the best proofs of condition. In this capture, from the time the fish was struck till I had him floundering on the bank, full forty minutes elapsed, I having noted time previous to making the first cast at the head of the pool.

On examining my tackle, I found that it had suffered considerably, particularly the fly, which not only had one of the hackles broken, but also the tinsel; I therefore stuck it carefully in the crown of my hat, and replaced it with another, intending in the evening, when comfortably seated in our snug cabin, to bring my pliers, scissors, vice, &c., into play, and construct its counterpart, being well satisfied that the combination of colour which in previous exploits had done me good service, was again destined to reap fresh laurels and further establish its reputation. The upper portion of the stream, and the only part I had so far fished, was now well rested; and while refreshing myself preparatory to making a third essay, several noble fish broke water in the immediate vicinity where I had hooked both of my trophies. From what I had already seen, I was convinced that magnificent sport was before me, and that I had at last arrived in the land of plenty—of salmon. There was a satisfaction in knowing this—a feeling I will not attempt to describe, a gratification of a longing often felt, but never expected to be realised. Fancy, brother fishermen, having salmon as abundant as trout in a good trout stream! In ten casts I had three rises, out of which I had hooked and killed two fish; and my friend across the water had also been busy—possibly five salmon taken out of one reach, and that within an hour and a half! Ye lords and commoners, who pay enormous rentals for salmon rivers, can you, with all the paraphernalia that a London fishing-tackle establishment can supply, with all the attendance and accessories that wealth can purchase, show a finer record? Truly I doubt if it is possible. Again I commenced at the head of the pool, and slowly progressed downwards; one fish I stirred, but on a second time casting over him, he refused to put in an appearance. Step after step I descended, and when not more than ten yards below where I had hooked my first fish, I struck another; but, alas! the hook did not hold; a few spasmodic struggles, and he was free. That I was too slow in striking I attribute as the cause; for at the moment I had observed a mink standing on a stone watching my proceedings with curious eye—no doubt wondering what kind of creature his optics, possibly for the first time, rested on. Of one thing I am certain — you cannot be too quick in striking salmon; they come up with such velocity that not a moment should be lost in responding to their call.

Salmon or trout fishing is not alone enjoyable for the pleasure of killing fish, but for the scenery and attachments which form the necessary adjuncts to the sport. The distance from the haunts of fellow men, the solitude of perhaps the surrounding forest, the soft murmuring of the descending and rushing water, the opportunity afforded to study nature in its unalloyed purity—all tend to enhance, to the true lover of nature, this princely sport; the very combination of all these *et ceteras* making the perfection, which all will acknowledge to belong to fly-fishing. During the noon hours I determined to remain behind, while my friend the skipper returned to his schooner, on the proviso that Jock should be landed with orders to report himself to me, to perform as gaffer for the evening's fishing; while the boat, at sundown, would come to the estuary to carry self and booty back for a late supper. As my friend departed, and the sullen plash of the oars, momentarily less distinct, told of increasing distance between me and mankind, my enjoyment of the scene became doubly enhanced by the depth of the solitude; and with full appreciation of the beautiful lines of Byron,—

northern latitudes, and much valued for its fur. The little episode was in keeping with what all who are observant of nature may daily witness—the stronger insect devouring the weaker, the more powerful animal the lesser, or man, the greatest tyrant of all, whatever falls within his reach, if worthy of the exertion, or suited to his fastidious palate.

The better to keep at bay the pestiferous bloodsuckers, I lit a cigar, and again lounged, trying to kill time, and pass as agreeably as possible the interval between Jock's arrival and my evening's fishing. About half-past two the boy came, and we both started for the upper pool. Already I had christened our scene of operations the upper, lower, and middle pool, and the stretch, which was a long rapid, connecting the two latter; so that, in speaking of them by these appellations, the reader will be aware to what portion I allude.

On reaching the water, although little after three o'clock, much to my satisfaction the fish were on the move, and during the few minutes that were necessary to arrange my tackle, over a dozen succeeded in ascending the shoot. It is seldom that the lover of nature can witness a more satisfactory and pleasing exhibition than that of salmon passing up a leap. Their efforts and perseverance are truly astonishing, and frequently dozens of essays will be made before one is successful. The manner of performing their ascent is a proof of the immense velocity, strength of body, and enormous power, with which they are gifted; from six to eight feet can be accomplished by them, and I have heard many persons assert more. When once the fish gain the summit over the edge of the upper bend, a few spasmodic, rapid motions of the tail carry them forward, and they disappear from view so suddenly as to leave the beholder in doubt whether they have succeeded, or been carried down in the surging fall.

The flies continued exceedingly troublesome, particularly a small species of sand-fly. So minute are they that when on your hand it is almost impossible to detect their exact situation; but however insignificant, their powers of torture are intense, for immediately after they have punctured the skin, a small water-blister rises, which smarts as acutely as a burn from the application of nitric acid.

All the concoctions that I have ever used to repel these pests have, so far, signally failed to give the desired relief; oil of pennyroyal, camphor, hartshorn, &c. &c., are useless, because their power evaporates the moment they are exposed to the atmosphere; fish-oil and oil of tar retain their virtue a little longer, but they require too frequent applications for one engaged in exciting sport, as well as being filthy and soiling to all you come in contact with, making your approach most objectionable to your companions, from the offensiveness of the smell. If some of our numerous ingenious chemists would set their brains to work and discover a practical means of repulsion of these vampires, they would earn the goodwill of all the followers of the gentle craft.

The fifth or sixth throw rose and hooked a fine fish, which made me uncommonly busy; he was remarkably lively, and kept me on the move the first ten minutes. I scarcely ever remember to have seen a salmon break water so frequently; after the first burst, with about sixty yards out, he showed himself six or seven times, springing on each occasion several feet clear of the surface. However, these exertions told upon my foe, for when I turned him he submitted to be guided till all surplus line was in. Through a stumble which I made on passing over the rocks, I accidentally checked him more abruptly than Mr. Salmon thought was courteous, for off again he went with the velocity of a steam-engine; however, my tackle was strong and hook well planted, and soon, a second time, I had him under control, and by exercising a little politeness of the give-and-take order, I brought him into shallow water. Jock, my faithful attendant, was by, and with intense delight waded into the stream. "Careful, boy! be cautious!" But all was thrown away; he made a grab at the fish with the gaff, as a sailor would with a boat-hook, but fortunately dragged the fish in water too shoal for swimming. Jock saw he had made a bungle, and was determined to retrieve if possible his lost reputation; he threw himself on the struggling salmon, and after a groping match of some minutes, with imminent danger to my tackle, proudly walked ashore, wet from head to foot, with the prize tightly cuddled up in his arms. Although at first tempted to anathematise the young scamp, I enjoyed a hearty laugh at the nonchalance with which the monkey treated his ducking.

Moving down the water, I recommenced operations and rose two good fish; soon I got fast to a third, which gave me ten minutes' splendid sport, then he sulked, and after two or three futile attempts to escape, succumbed. I was surprised at obtaining so easy a victory, but this was explained by finding a piece cut out of his back, in front of the first dorsal fin, upwards of an inch in width, and two or three long. In trout fishing, I have once or twice taken fish similarly wounded, and as there were no gill nets at either place, the only satisfactory reason I can attribute is, that either a seal or an otter was the perpetrator.

As the evening advanced I changed flies, and selected what I have long known by the sobriquet of "the drummer;" it is composed thus: the mottled feathers of the peacock's wing, with a few strands of golden pheasant for wings; body, light brown fur of the bear next the hide, mixed with orange-sable fur and gold-coloured mohair; gold tinsel, loosely but regularly wrapped with blood or claret coloured hackle round the shoulder, and ordinary red hackle lower down. This fly has always been with me a great favourite, more particularly if the water is clearing out after rain, and with confidence I recommend it; at the same time I would have two or three sizes, the choice to be dictated by the size of water, colour, and hour. Some persons, in addition, have forked it with two or three hairs of the squirrel for tail; and a very worthy friend and admirable fly-fisher, whose success was a guarantee of his skill, used to affirm, that when fish wouldn't rise at "the drummer," you might as well go bed. As the results will show, my couch was not put in requisition, for ere many minutes I touched a splendid fish, but unfortunately didn't hold him. After a few minutes without success, I moved a very heavy fish without touching him. Again I gave him a chance, and he tumbled over the fly like a porpoise, without any apparent inclination to take. The third time that I offered, however, I was more successful, for in striking I hooked the fish foul. The result was curious and far from satisfactory, for this fellow put me through a course of spurts which opened my optics, and further convinced me of the uncertainty of the movements or plan of escape that is probable to be adopted by the impaled. What was my surprise—and I am confident many others would have been similarly affected—to see my victim remain on the surface, not jumping out of the stream, but beating the water with his tail, and violently struggling, making the liquid fly for feet around. For several moments this continued, when, changing operations, down stream he went with surprising velocity. The reel screeched, and I followed with agile and careful steps, when,—confound it! the d—l take it!—readers, you must excuse, remember the aggravation—my rod broke at the ferrule of the second joint, and my line returned to my feet like a coil of rope scientifically thrown by an expert boatman. I was in despair. Such damage could not be repaired where I then was; my leader and new fly were gone, possibly for the estuary of the St. Lawrence, and, like a vessel stranded in a falling tide, I was perfectly helpless. To find the cause of this unexpected casualty was my first endeavour. The wood of the rod at the fracture looked fresh and sound, the brass appeared to be put on correctly, but there was something to be discovered yet of which I was still ignorant, and to the reel I went to solve the problem. In winding up or taking in line I had, through carelessness, permitted one round to lap across the other. In paying away the two had jammed, coming to a full stop. My rod had been broken, my fly stolen, and my casting line was probably performing duty for a pennant to a fish totally disregarding distance or trespass. "There's no use grieving over spilt milk," some one says, and after I had got rid of the fizz, like a bottle of soda-water, I was calm enough, only regretting I had lost the salmon, for, with all fishermen, the fish that gets off is, of course, a very great deal larger than any you have captured.

To be a perfect fisherman you require more excellences than are usually to be found in such a small space as is allotted to man's carcass; you should be patient, forbearing, vigorous, decided and prompt in emergency, with the constitution of a water-spaniel, and the ingenuity of an Arkwright or a Fulton. Being deficient in many, more particularly in the latter requisites, I was compelled to shut up shop by putting up my rod in its canvas covering, regretting my bad luck, my stupidity, and last, though not least, the fish that had worsted me at my own game. Not being in the best of humour, of course Jock was out of the way and not within hailing distance. What a capital chance to vent the balance of my spleen, not at all improved by the confounded flies, whose attacks, since I had ceased to be employed, became more noticeable; in truth, if it were possible, I doubt not that I should have liked to saddle the boy with his absence being the cause of my mishaps. After several times shouting his name he at length appeared, hat in hand, bareheaded, with a smile of childlike satisfaction on his face that, even in my irate state, I had not the heart to destroy. To my inquiry where he had been, with a look of satisfaction he informed me he had found and harried a nest, producing his hat full of the stolen treasures. After giving him a lecture on the impropriety of such a course, and the probabilities of his being devoured by wolves and bears, or even cannibals, if he left my side, I could not help making an inspection of what his bonnet contained. Truly he had a hat full, for upwards of a dozen pale cinnamon blotched eggs, a trifle larger than those of the domestic pigeon, lay at the bottom. The nest and parent bird, from description, left me in no doubt that Master Jock had deprived some luckless Rock Ptarmigan (*Lagopus albus*) of her embryo brood; and after lecturing him on the enormity of such a proceeding, and begging a share of the spoils, we started for the place of rendezvous.

The evening after my first day's sport was not an idle one, for though the body inclined to rest, full well I knew that on my exertions in fly-tying depended the sport of to-morrow. To make a good fly requires not only skill, but patience and knowledge, with a correct taste in the blending of colours; a strong hand, to make secure work, and the employment of the best materials. How frequently indifferent hooks and gut are purchased because they are a trifle cheaper; but if we could foresee the severe ordeal that may some day be in store for our tackle, and the splendid fish that may be lost through this want of judgment, we should be better suited with half the quantity at double the cost. Your feathers should, if possible, be fresh, with the pile unbroken; your furs and mohair uncut by moths, and your silk the strongest, yet the finest that can be procured. Of course many of your principal feathers will require to be purchased, but if the fisherman is also a shooter, there are few game birds that will not afford him choice materials; so that during autumn and winter, when his gun, instead of rod, is his companion, he can daily make additions to his treasures, which will serve him in pursuing the sister amusement.

Everything which makes deception more alluring should be resorted to by an angler; for, let his experience be ever so great, he will always find opportunities to regret his deficiencies. Where all depends so much upon chance, it is impossible to see the disadvantages under which you may frequently labour, or the awkward positions in which you may occasionally be placed; where it is absolutely necessary for the fisherman to put on an unusual and severe strain to turn a hooked fish, so as to prevent his going over some surging fall, or down or up stream, inaccessible to the steps of the angler. Sometimes, of course, the loss of fish, or even fish and tackle, cannot be avoided; but good, careful work, and the best materials, will frequently obviate so annoying an ordeal. However, having struck your fish, the tackle and your own coolness are generally responsible for the issue, and woe betide you if careless knot or indifferent tying should have been made in constructing your leader or fly.

I would therefore advise all gentlemen to acquaint themselves thoroughly with the method of their construction, for though they may not have time and inclination to follow it as a pursuit, they may chance to be placed in positions where their pleasure and the success of their expedition may be entirely marred by want of this knowledge.

I would further advise that your leaders should be stained as nearly as possible to the colour of the water; but care should always be taken not to make them too dark, as you thus go to the opposite extreme that you adopt this plan to avoid. Brown and a bluish grey or light neutral tint are decidedly the best colours, the former to be used when the water is clearing out after heavy falls of rain. To procure the first-mentioned colour, a few ounces of alum dissolved with a pound of the bark of the walnut tree when the sap is up, I think is the simplest recipe; while the latter colour can be got by substituting logwood for walnut.

Of course, as the season advances, and the quantity of water diminishes, and the noonday sun becomes more powerful, the size of your flies must be proportionably less. Even the hours of the day have to be consulted for choice of size; for instance, from break of day till sunrise and from sunset till dark, very large flies frequently will take, while the smaller would be totally neglected.

An Irish gentleman, who had for many years been considered one of the most successful and expert performers on the river Corib, while on a fishing tour in America, had the kindness to show me the treasures contained in his valuable fly-book. Among a remarkably choice collection of all sizes, shades, and construction I observed many so large that they excited my curiosity and inquiry. Some were several inches long in the body, and were commonly used in Galway for early morning or late evening fishing.

Those projecting an excursion to the distant wilds of Labrador should pay particular attention to arriving there at the correct season. As to specifying a day or a week, that is perfectly impossible, for as long as the water is impregnated with snow not a fish will be taken; and, of course, the lateness or earliness of spring, which frequently varies one or two weeks, must receive consideration and guide your steps. The first few days after the salmon commence to run flies of a large size are more successful, but as the season advances their size must be reduced.

The next morning, bright and early, found us again upon the river. The number of seals which I had seen the previous evening induced me to take my rifle, with the intention of having a little practice during the noonday rest. The rocks in the estuary appeared a perfect nursery of these curious animals, and from their numbers and well-known destructive habits, immense quantities of salmon must be annually destroyed to satisfy their fastidious and insatiable appetites. I have since found out that the Habitants (persons of French extraction) frequently pay visits to this *locale* for the capture of these valuable Amphibia, their oil and skins fetching long prices in our principal markets. Since yesterday the water had fallen some inches, but I had little fear that where fish were so numerous and little disturbed it would unfavourably affect their disposition to take. Having faith in the fly I designated "the drummer," I determined to experimentalise with others, retaining my old friend as a last resource in case of failure. I therefore selected a former favourite, known by many as "the hornet," and whose texture and shape had produced good results in many localities. The fly is made as follows: wings from the fine fibres of the English cock pheasant's tail; body of yellow worsted or amber-coloured mohair, the mohair to be preferred; the body to be ribbed with black and made full, with a large red cock's hackle, black at the roots, wrapped several times under the butt of the wings. Having got my rod together I commenced work, and the success which had attended my efforts of the day before and my choice of flies were quite equalled by this day's performance. The third cast I rose a superb fish, but, unfortunately, scratched him, and had the same misfortune repeated before many minutes. However, by the time I had got thirty yards down the water, I struck another, whose unusual size and activity evoked unlimited admiration. His first rush was truly magnificent, and as soon as I succeeded in stopping his precipitous course, he returned almost to my hand with the same velocity, preventing my immediately recovering the slack of my line. From pleasure a moment before, I was now nearly in grief, and but for luck should certainly have lost my prize. However, being thus favoured, I got again upon equal terms. A quarter of an hour more and the gaff pierced his silver coat of mail, and I had the satisfaction of capturing a handsome and well-made fourteen-pound fish.

That morning I killed eight fish, the majority weighing about nine pounds, and the number I rose and touched must have been quite equal. One salmon I rose six times in succession, but ultimately failed to secure: from the swirl he left in the water, I should imagine he was about fifteen pounds. On my way down to the tideway I observed two new specimens of birds, whose plaintive notes were very sweet; their names I have never been able to ascertain, but doubtlessly they belong to the numerous bunting family. Crossbills, snow-birds, and cedar-birds were abundantly numerous; and, although I did not succeed in obtaining any of their nests, I am convinced that they were engaged in rearing families, as I perceived several gathering grubs and insects, with which they flew to the neighbouring brush.

Having got to the boat, we started for the reef to

try what could be done with the seals. But they did not like our appearance, and commenced scuffling off the rocks and dropping into the water ere we got within range; however, one old scoundrel—grim and savage-looking through age—appeared less alarmed than his fellows, and remained stationary, watching our motions with dubious eyes. When within fifty yards the men ceased pulling, and permitted the boat to forge ahead with her own way. Pulling the tiller lines so as to alter the course, I got a clean shot, and turned the ungainly, awkward brute over; but his struggles carried him down the incline till he fell in the water, when he sunk immediately. After much difficulty we managed to get him out, and, on examination, found the ball had pierced the skull a little over the right eye. His weight must have been upwards of three hundred pounds, and the quantity of grease that came from the carcass, as we divested him of his pelt, was surprising. The hide of these animals makes most excellent shoes when properly tanned, and I have been told that nothing in the shape of leather is so capable of turning water. One shot was sufficient to expel the seals from their haunt, so we returned shoreward; however, just as we were about to land, a youngster popped up his head, which I let drive at, but without precision.

The flies to-day continued very annoying, and the irritation caused by their bites itched so severely, that it affected the majority of our tempers; the only respite that could be obtained was when out on the water, where the draught of air had full scope. Oh, that some one, versed in the likings and dislikes of these insidious foes, would find a method that would protect the angler from these pests, when he is enjoying a trip that has no other drawbacks. To describe my sufferings would be impossible; suffice it to say, that my actions were sufficient to cause a physician to imagine me fit for incarceration in a lunatic asylum; even now I can scarcely revert to the subject without feeling irritated.

Revenons à nos moutons. With salmon fishing, the imaginary moment of victory is frequently the precursor of defeat; the noble adversary but relaxes his efforts that, in the resulting confidence which follows, he may the more successfully concentrate his powers for a final dash, that frequently results as I have shown. I can compare it to nought else than the skilful swordsman, who, finding himself overmatched in his antagonist, gives ground and feigns fatigue to imbue his foe with confidence, hoping that a careless pass will still afford him an opportunity to deliver the deadly thrust. Men have always foibles, always paramount pleasures; their tastes are as diversified as the colouring in Joseph's coat, as the physiognomy which we bear. While one is devoted to the horse, another is to the hound; while one loves the gun, another loves the rod; to question their tastes and argue with them the reason, would probably be unproductive, but of this I am convinced, no man ever felt the pleasure, the intense excitement of having a salmon on a rod, or even the more diminutive trout, without being again desirous of renewing the sensation; the very uncertainty causes this fascination. A gentleman for whom I have much esteem, and who has been busily employed all his life in mercantile pursuits, principally abroad and in countries where fly-fishing was not practicable, a few years ago met me on a fishing excursion. His essays with the fly, from lack of experience, were not generally successful; but when I hooked a heavy fish and handed him the rod to play the deluded victim, his countenance, particularly if victorious, exhibited more satisfaction than I believe it would have done if he had made thousands of dollars. Fishing—legitimate fishing with rod and fly—requires but to be known and practised to have more votaries than any other sport extant.

That afternoon I killed four more fish, all worthy of

a place in the memory of the most successful angler, all deserving of notice for their plucky efforts to avoid their doom. But numbers have satiated my memory, and their efforts, ruses, and struggles cease to occupy a place in my retrospect; for the gallant fight of the salmon that you have been fortunate enough to impale —unless his exertions are marked by some new device or specialty in the conflict—lives no longer in the memory than kindnesses do in that of many. How many strive after a prize, use all their efforts and energy to be so successful as to obtain it, and how often, when successful, they throw the coveted treasure on one side, as if no longer worthy of possession! I much fear that such is as often the case with the disciples of the gentle art, as with those who follow less fascinating pleasures.

Just as I was thinking of closing up for the night, my companion shouted to me that there was a bear in the water; on looking up stream, sure enough there was bruin, stemming the current and boldly pushing for this side. With hasty impulse I laid my rod down to grasp my rifle, but, alas! my attendant, fatigued with carrying it, and seeing small prospect of its being required, had left it leaning against a rock some distance off. You may well imagine my disappointment, for when the bear left the water he was not over twenty-five yards above my position. This animal, judging from his size, must have been quite four hundred pounds—a size much greater than it generally attains in the north-west. Until he had firmly gained his footing he had not observed us, and the ludicrousness of his alarm and astonishment when he became aware of our vicinity was laughable in the extreme. Off he went with a rush into the brush, making dry and withered limbs crash before him.

As the constant and severe attentions of the flies put a nap out of the question, and I had become surfeited with tobacco from the number of cigars I had consumed, under the fallacy that the smoke would deprive me of their company, I was compelled as a last resource to start on a tour of inspection; at the same time hoping that my exertions would be rewarded with the discovery of some quadruped or bird with which I had been previously unacquainted. On entering the scrub bush the mosquitoes became more numerous, and I have little hesitation in saying, that the bloodsuckers of Arkansas and Mississippi, which bear the same name, are far from proficients when you compare them with those of Labrador. After half an hour's rough scrambling through the morass, I succeeded in gaining more open ground. Rising towards the upper ridges of high lands, the squawberry and blueberry grew in profusion, and the wild strawberry was scattered in patches wherever sufficient sustenance from the impoverished soil could be gained for its support. In straying about I found two nests of the night hawk, and both of different plumage from those I have so frequently seen of a summer evening on the banks of the Ohio River; the eggs in both were four in number, of a dirty colour, smudged with brown, and almost lying on the bare rock. This bird is doubtlessly migratory, resorting here in summer for the purpose of propagation, and spending its winters in the more genial climate of the Southern States, where it changes its plumage to one of less brilliancy and receives the local appellation of "bull bat."

In the rocks and sand I found some fossils of shells, and on such elevated ground that it caused me at the time surprise and wonder whether shell-fish were once denizens of land instead of water, or whether these mountains had once been submerged. Hares appeared to be numerous, as their paths crossed and recrossed each other, forming a perfect labyrinth. Ptarmigan and the Canada partridge I also saw so frequently, that I have little doubt, in the month of September, fine sport might be obtained with dog and gun. Bear signs were also abundant, a solitary stump showing evidence of the power of their claws, and from the height some of these convincing proofs extended up its side, the bruin family are evidently not stunted in growth in this locality.* After walking for almost an hour, I succeeded in reaching the crest of one of the numerous swells, and, as I turned to survey the scenery, one of the most enchanting panoramas that ever I witnessed broke upon my vision. Bays and arms of the sea, innumerable small islands, numerous reefs of rocks and uncountable mountain peaks stretched as far as the eye could see; while almost beneath my feet lay our goodly little schooner, reduced by distance to a mere cockle-shell,—the busy crew passing to and fro upon the beach, looked scarcely larger than ants. Here, with the unobstructed breeze playing upon me, I got a little peace from the troublesome insects, and I would have remained longer but that the hour indicated the close proximity of the time to commence my evening fishing.

The fly I had used in the morning had done me such good service that I determined to re-employ it, and the result was quite equal to anticipation. I soon got to work, and in a few minutes was fast in a fine fish, who, although he made a noble struggle,

---

* In every locality where bears are numerous, all appear to select the same tree to try their claws upon. Of course the larger bears make the highest incisions. From these marks an expert hunter can form a good estimate of the size of the visitors.

succumbed in less than twenty minutes. Moving my position from some slow water, I took a cast in the throat of a stream formed by the projection of some rocks, not that I expected to rise a fish, but to get the line out of my way as I scrambled over some rough ground; in fact the water, although rapid, looked too shallow for the retreat of anything over a pound weight. With surprise I rose a fine brook trout (*Salmo fontinalis*). Of course such a fish was not to be despised, so I gave him a second chance, and had the satisfaction of succeeding in striking him. With my strong tackle and rod I treated him cavalierly, and, in about ten minutes, had the pleasure of handling and canvassing his weight, which was a trifle over five pounds.

I never remember to have seen a fish of more brilliant colouring and beautiful proportions, and I have little doubt that on a seven-ounce trout-rod he would have given a good half-hour's pleasure. These streams —or those which lie in this portion of the American continent—swarm with trout, more particularly when you ascend some distance above the tideway; and from information I have received from fishermen who are acquainted with those waters that lie nearer to civilisation, I have reason to believe that brook trout can there be caught upwards of ten pounds in weight.

Moving down to the run, I recommenced, and rose a very large fish the second cast; but our acquaintance got no further, for all my blandishments were futile to induce him again to move. A little lower down I was more successful, for I struck a regular Trojan, whose memory still lives, and to whose performances I award the palm over all others. As soon as he felt himself pricked, contrary to the custom of his brethren in a similar predicament, he rushed up stream with the velocity of a bullet, through the throat of surging water and into the next pool; fortunately the ground was accessible, and I was enabled to follow, but for the life of me I could not, dared not, take a pull on him. From the fish's movements I should think he was swimming about two feet deep, and, from the power and speed that he showed, appeared totally to ignore any control. However, it's a straight road that has no turn, and if I was led a dance in the first instance, my turn was coming. After walking two hundred yards and giving out nearly one hundred yards of line, the drag told, and my friend thought it better to change his course; down stream he came with a rush, still without showing, but just as he got to the smooth, oily-like water that preceded the break of the rapid, he commenced springing with great rapidity. Five or six times this ruse was repeated, when off again my gallant foe went down stream, with as much energy and spirit as he had at first displayed. Well, to make a long story short, to and fro we both went, up and down, first one way and then another, till the fun became hard work, and the exertion caused globules of perspiration to stand on my face, and worse than all, the confounded flies attacked me with renewed vigour, availing themselves of my unprotected situation. Again and again I took in line,—as frequently to be run out; but the exertion had told on the foe, and at length I succeeded in getting him into shoal water. Truly he was a beauty—twenty pounds if an ounce—and already I felt that he was mine. Soon the silver sides alternately showed, and all that was wanted was a skilful gaffer. My man, however, did not prove himself so; he got directly between me and the fish—made an awkward attempt—managed in some unaccountable manner to get the line under his arm, which he had previously tried to take hold of, and made a stumble that alarmed the salmon, which, with a violent plunge, summoned all his energy and made again for the deep water, taking away the hook and part of my leader.

With regret, after supper that evening, I heard the captain state that he had made up his mind to be off on the morrow, for well I knew it was more than improbable that I should ever wet my line in such another salmon river. The number of fish I had killed was not so extraordinary, for I had not entirely devoted myself to the sport, had bad luck in breaking tackle, and lay off for many hours during the middle of each day; however, here there was no fear of a jealous antagonist cutting in before you, flogging your favourite pool, or, perhaps, on your arrival, finding him fast in the only fish in the river at that time on the feed.

If there is one thing in the world more trying than another to a man's temper, it is the above misfortune; and I often fear that though the tongue be tipped with courtesy and politeness, very far from amicable feelings are dominant in the heart; but because a favourite resort has just been threshed over, that is no reason you should not make an essay. Salmon are fastidious and fickle, and possibly the allurements you can offer will please their ideas more than all the blandishments of the first visitor. An acquaintance, not long ago, told me the following, which will prove the truth of the above. Some years since he was disappointed on arriving on his fishing ground, by finding one of the most successful anglers hard at work. Disheartened, perhaps, but not discouraged from making a trial, he put his rod together and commenced operations, the result of which was, that in a short time he had three fine fish, whereas his antagonist had not obtained a single rise. Nevertheless, I would much prefer to be the first to pass over the ground, or rather water, in spite of all that can be said to the contrary.

The last evening little else was done but fight our battles over again, and the number of cigar stumps and diminished bottles clearly bespoke the length of our sitting, and the relish we had for one another's conversation. A happier night I don't think I ever spent; and even now I look back to those few delightful days with unfeigned delight. Before retiring we settled that till noon on the morrow we would fish, and get under way as soon after as possible, both being repugnant to tear ourselves away from a locality which had afforded us so much pleasure.

With break of day on the morrow we were again reseated in our boat, starting for the river on our parting visit. The captain put out two lines astern with the hope of catching some hungry straggler of the deep, nor did the lines long remain idle; one in particular, which was attached to a large-sized Buell spoon, was kept constantly at work, and on two occasions it had scarce got well clear of the boat before it was seized. Several whales and innumerable porpoises kept plung-

P

ing on either side; one of the latter, of a pink, salmon colour,* rose so close to the boat as almost to be within reach of the oars. In the mouth of the river several sea-trout were taken, one a splendid fellow nearly six pounds. At first when he was struck, we thought it was a salmon from the rush he made, but soon after his spring from the water told us that our adversary was only first cousin to the king of game fish. On arrival at the place of disembarkation, the colour of the river pleased me much, being scarcely as clear as the day before, possibly caused by a shower up country, or some light slate-coloured clouds that floated in the westward heavens. As I marched up the course of the stream, I found not less than a dozen seals having a grand pow-wow, and with the hope of learning something of the habits of these strange Amphibia, or their method of catching their prey, I watched them from behind a rock; but the appearance of the captain on the other side of the stream, who was unaware of my *ruse*, put them all to rout like a flock of scared sheep; nor did they again show themselves till they were several hundred yards down the river.

I have never been able to learn to my satisfaction, from books or friends, how these ungainly creatures catch their prey, more especially when I know with what

* White porpoise, common in many parts of the world.

swiftness a hooked salmon can swim even with the strain of a powerful rod and stiff reel to impede his progress; and again, who, that has ever witnessed a fresh run salmon endeavouring to divest himself of sea-lice, can doubt for a moment that if the fish does not become charmed or entranced so as to paralyse his powers of locomotion, in a race he could far outstrip his awkward and ungainly foe. That seals prey upon salmon, and that to an enormous extent, is beyond a doubt, but how they succeed in capturing them is to me still a mystery.

On arriving at the upper pool I found the water perfectly boiling with fish; up, down, or across, wherever you cast your eyes, you could either see the dark back of a salmon or the splash made by its plunge. This symptom, I am inclined to believe, is frequently ominous of bad sport, as fish will play in the manner described before a fall of rain, and at the same time will totally disregard the most alluring fly that can be fabricated. In trout-fishing, particularly, I have found this to be the case. One evening, a few years since, when on a fishing excursion in Northern Maine, the show of fish was immense, and the water being perfectly smooth permitted every break to be seen. The forenoon had been unusually warm, in fact the atmosphere felt as if surcharged with electricity, and consequently I had determined to fish no more that day; still this extraordinary show caused me to break my resolution; but far better had I stayed at home, for two hours were spent fruitlessly, scarcely having killed a single fish; when, under ordinary circumstances, on the same pools, I could have doubly filled my basket. However, this want of success was soon explained, for that evening, an hour after sunset, one of the most severe thunder-storms I ever witnessed took place. A New Yorker, whose fly-book I had the pleasure of lately examining,—the contents of which included the most perfectly tied trout-flies I ever saw, and who was reported to be as skilful in handling the rod as he was in making dubbing and feathers represent an insect,—informed me that he could always tell by the barometer when fish would feed well; now, this is a novel use to put this instrument to.

But to my story. I commenced fishing with sanguine expectations, and the issue was commensurate. The third cast I hooked and killed a ten-pounder. Again I went to work, and before many minutes was fast to another, which, after the first run, unfortunately escaped, my hold doubtlessly being a bad one. Nothing daunted by the mishap, I was soon again firm in a third fish, and from the strain and headlong force of the rush, doubtless a good one—twenty pounds if an ounce—and such he proved when he broke water, with every prospect of success; for I consider the first burst, until the fish is turned, as far more dangerous and probable to result in disaster than any other portion of the fray. At least an hour did I give to gain the victory; but as I brought my prize, now thoroughly exhausted, into shoal water, I felt that I would sooner have undergone five times the labour and loss of time than lose my fish. With repeated cautions, my attendant entered the water, the same man who had accompanied me the first day, and using his gaff with the proficiency of one who had served a long apprenticeship, skilfully landed the salmon at the first attempt. This one when weighed barely turned twenty pounds, and was, by long odds, the finest that was captured by either myself or the skipper.

As I passed down the comparatively stagnant portion of the pool, an indication of current that eddied round a point of rock in the centre of the river particularly struck me as being a place worthy of attention. Easing out a few extra yards of line so as to throw above and beyond it, I made a cast, and almost simultaneously two fine fish dashed at the fly, but without success. At the second cast I was more successful, for I hooked a salmon, which I landed in a very short time. Although this fish had all the appearances of being fresh run he afforded very little sport, and but that he was well-formed, solid, and had not lost the sea-lice, I should have been inclined to believe that he was a spent fish. As such an occurrence has happened to me before, I think that the most satisfactory elucidation is that he had just arrived in fresh water, and had not had time to recover from the fatigue of his journey.

The afternoon of the first day of my visit Master Jock had amused himself catching chub, and, boy-like, had made a *cache* in the sand in which he deposited about a couple of dozen. On passing this spot I found that it had been visited by bears the previous night, who had devoured all the results of the lad's prowess. From the footprints left on the sand, I concluded that the bruin party consisted of an old lady and a couple of young hopefuls. Doubtless good sport could be had here trapping. A few properly-constructed bowers, with hanging baits and good traps, would give the hunter abundant and remunerative employment.

At the head of the run I recommenced fishing, and in less than ten minutes had struck and risen three beauties; but, unfortunately, the gentleman I hooked, in the first exhibition of his disgust at being so egregiously sold, returned the compliment and victimised me by taking away a portion of my leader and the fly. The hornet so far had done my morning's work, and not having a second, I mounted the drummer; the alteration in choice was not detrimental, for at the seventh or eighth cast I hooked a handsome fellow, who after a well-contested battle struck his colours. On moving downwards, I almost placed my foot on a duck with a numerous progeny. Depositing my rod carefully, I started in pursuit. Though scarcely as fleet as a greyhound, I have a tolerably long pair of useful legs, but although I put them to the best use, it was all of no avail: the little bunches of fluff and down fairly ran me to a standstill. Several times I tried to throw myself on them, but their agility and marvellous powers of dodging,—first squatting in one tuft of grass, then in another,—forced me to give up the contest. A few minutes after, I saw the whole party, under their parent's guidance, making their best exertions to reach the opposite shore. This duck was of a variety to me entirely new, about the size of the wood duck, but entirely different in colouring. The nearest approach to it I know of is a water-fowl known on the Ohio and Wabash rivers as winter duck or whistler, the difference of plumage possibly being caused by the season.

Four more salmon I killed that morning, making, as I think our friends will agree, a handsome forenoon's work; but as the sun was becoming very powerful, and with its increased heat the confounded flies were again attentive, with more than ordinary repugnance I determined to unlimber, hoping that Providence, in her kindness, would at some future day land me on the solitary shores of this picturesque and admirably-adapted river for pursuing with success and ease the ever-fascinating, ever-changing, ever-exciting, gentlemanly sport of salmon fishing.

By one o'clock we weighed anchor, and after a few tacks got out into open water, where a favourable breeze quickly carried us from a spot that will ever hold a bright, happy impression in my memory; and as the sun set in golden, refulgent splendour, a low line of distant, indistinct, bluish hills, were the only visible marks in the horizon that remained to indicate where the choicest river on which I had ever wetted a fly rolled its pellucid, sparkling water to the all-absorbing ocean.

My friend, the captain, I have not met since we parted at Russell's Hotel, Quebec (where he was obliged to go for repairs), after drinking to auld lang syne and future meetings; but a year since I heard that fortune had smiled upon him, and that he had returned to the land of Burns, amply provided to enjoy peace and plenty for the rest of his days, and give some comfort, as he used to say, "to the gude auld folks." *

* During my visit to America last winter, I was presented by Livingston Stone, Esq., with five hundred pregnate ova of American salmon, which I forwarded to Frank Buckland, Esq., Commissioner of her Majesty's Fisheries. They are now to be seen in the Museum of Economic Fish Culture at South Kensington. Introducing new blood, even among fish, may be found beneficial.

CHAPTER XIV.

THE PRONG-HORNED ANTELOPE.

(*Antilocapra Americana.*)

THIS is the only species of the genus, and is about the size of *Cervus Virginianus*, graceful and elegant in form and action, and probably as swift as any known quadruped. Well may the Americans be proud of possessing the only representative of the race, and truly with good reason. When the antelope is seen on the boundless prairies of the Far West, untrammelled by limit, free to go and return as they choose, the impressions caused will never be effaced, or a better representation of perfect independence and freedom beheld. It is with sorrow I state that the limits of this beautiful creature are day by day becoming more and more contracted, and predict that, with the bison (*Bos Americanus*) and the Indian, it will ere long cease to exist, save in the memory of those who knew these princely hunting-grounds before the intruding, grasping white race scattered themselves over what had been sacred and free from their intrusion. I do not love my own race less, but at the same time cannot deny that there is a pleasure on the boundless plain, the dense forest, when you can commune with yourself alone, and say, "I am the first of my nation who has ever penetrated or stood upon this spot. And then the precursors of civilisation, however capable they may be of breaking up soil, felling timber, and splitting rails, are of all society the least qualified to be thrown among the representatives of the aboriginal animals, for they slay without discretion, slaughter for the sake of shedding blood, are more bloodthirsty than the wolf or panther, and only cease when all are exterminated or banished from their vicinity.

The prong-horned antelope is in height about three feet at the shoulder, over four feet from tail to termination of nose, smaller in the ear than the *Cervus* family, while the beautifully sabre-curved prong-horn is from six to eight inches in length. The colour on the back, down the thighs and hips, is dark brown; the stomach, throat, and exterior side of ham a yellowish white, while a distinct dark bar, like a collar, girds the throat, eight or ten inches below the setting on of the head. The eye is large, soft, and protruding; nostrils extended, and the ears stand usually horizontal, and are very pointed. The limbs are tall in proportion to the animal's height, excessively muscular in make, and strongly indicative of the immense velocity with which it can travel. So great is this animal's speed that I feel confident in saying that neither greyhound nor racehorse would have the slightest chance to overtake it on any description of tolerably firm soil. The Indians catch them generally by making a surround, when the squaws enjoy the honour of the slaughtering. Hundreds are frequently taken in this manner. Again, they are sometimes captured by frightening them into the snowdrifts; but, after all, the greatest numbers fall a prey to their own curiosity. To stalk within gunshot of the prong-horn is at all times difficult; they are gifted with the most acute senses of hearing and smelling, and once alarmed but a short space of time will elapse before they have placed miles between themselves and the intruder; but if the hunter approach up wind within two or three hundred yards of his prey, carefully conceal himself, draw his ramrod, and on it place a boot, cap, or piece of rag, and describe eccentric rotary motions through the air, the unsuspicious but curiosity-excited beauties will soon observe the novel machine, and keep gradually approaching, till they will frequently come so close that the swarthy redskin can without fail pierce them with an arrow.

As food, when young, they are excellent; when old,

unless hung for a long time, the flesh is tough and stringy, although well-flavoured, having a peculiar gamey flavour not unlike hare.

The sexes can be distinguished by the inferiority of height in the female, by the horns being only prickers without the prong, and by the absence of mane, which the male when in winter pelage possesses of considerable size.

These animals at one time were found abundant as soon as the great plains were reached that lay westward of the Mississippi; now, however, their eastern limit is much farther off towards the Rocky Mountains, while from Northern Mexico to fifty-two or fifty-three degrees north latitude, may be asserted as their northern and southern bounds. From their being at home in, or indigenous to, so large an extent of country, where every temperature can be felt, from the heat of Africa to the cold of Siberia, it seems that they are well worth attention for acclimatisation. If this be not done they will soon cease to exist, and what a reproach it would be that an animal so beautiful, graceful, and appropriate for our parks should pass away without a representative.

I am now making efforts to procure some of these antelopes. I hope soon to be able to report success, for I should truly feel proud if I were the instrument by which they became adopted as fit inhabitants for our parks and demesnes.

In referring to my diary, I find the following narrative of a day's shooting:—

"Cap., are you asleep?" such was the welcome sound that informed me that some one else was awake besides myself. Such a night I do not think I had ever previously passed, and trust shall never have to again. To ask a man nurtured in a Christian land whether he was asleep!—the thing is perfectly preposterous: a gale of wind blowing the entire night, with drops of rain as large and so numerous that a brick wall would scarcely have repelled them, let alone a flimsy break-wind composed of green boughs, yet these western companions of mine slept! Half-a-dozen times I determined to rout my companions out, and as often gave up the idea; for one was quarrelsome whenever his rest was disturbed, the other had a disagreeable way of telling the most doleful stories, and keeping the listeners in a constant state of excitement, for in every shadow, every movement of the horses, every unusual sound, he saw an indication that a whole tribe of Indians, fully decked with war-paint, and thirsting for scalps, were about to make an onslaught on our defenceless bivouac. Further, I must inform my readers that Cap. is an abbreviation of captain, used all over the western portion of the United States, for every man who has borne arms, whether in the militia or regulars; whether he has been a full private or only a camp follower. Yes, I was awake, as wide awake as a pool of water under each arm, each knee, and every protuberant portion of the figure could make me. With an anathema against weather, country, and out-door life, I sprang up, and willingly busied myself in raking together the fragments of what had been a fire; long and tedious were the efforts to coax a blaze, but at length the reward of patience was vouchsafed, and in spite of the almost insurmountable obstacles a sufficient heat was obtained, by which we could cook the *débris* of last night's supper, the sole remnants of provisions the larder could boast of.

At the time to which I allude we were on a branch or small fork that flowed into the Pawnee River from the south. I and my companions had come from the westward, and had experienced as hard a time as it is possible to conceive; we had been about two weeks together, and although I am doubtful of the propriety of picking up strange acquaintances when beyond civilisation, those squeamish ideas never enter the heads of western *habitués;* a white man is always a friend until he proves himself to be otherwise, and then it is your own look-out that he does not get the upper hand. Wild life makes you wonderfully wide awake, and although an appparent *bonhommie* may lay on the surface, a constant guarded caution should never be neglected. My friends, however, were really good fellows, a little eccentric, for each was in the habit of picking his teeth with his bowie knife; but they were honest, plucky, and enduring, ready to face whatever emergency occurred, and pretty certain to get out of it if a bold hand and quick eye could be of assistance. Breakfast! what a misnomer for a few mouthfuls of half-charred, half-cooked, pieces of tough venison! what a contrast with one of our home hunting-feeds that bear the same *sobriquet;* still I doubt much whether *patés de fois gras*, game pies, and spiced round of beef, were ever relished with more gusto than that meal.

After the viands had disappeared, over the consoling, soothing pipe, our course for the day was discussed, and, as the rain had ceased and clouds lifted, giving every prospect of fine weather, it was decided that we should remain another night where we were, and in the meantime each start in different directions to seek for a supply of game, that we might not go supperless to rest and resume our journey on the morrow with empty stomachs. I had a horse; from his wonderful formation and intense ugliness I dubbed him " Broomstick ;" he was truly a doleful beast to look at; no amount of food seemed to do him any good; he always appeared in the last stage of consumption, although his capacity of stowage of forage was immense; nor did he ever lose a chance to get a cow kick at the unwary, or make his teeth meet in the flesh of the too confiding. Broomstick, from having lately had a very easy time, was selected for the day's work, and with expressions of grief that would break the heart of the most obdurate, he submitted to be saddled up, I returning every few minutes to take an extra pull upon the girths, for the villain would expand himself like a bull frog that had fallen into the hands of unfeeling schoolboys, so that when you imagined you had got safely seated and ready to start, by a succession of the most mulish and awkward back-jumps, the saddle would get forward beyond where his withers ought to have been, and nought but wonderful skill or fortune in the laws of equitation would prevent the rider from kissing mother-earth. Now Broomstick could go if you knew how to take it out of him, and that was accomplished by commencing with a high hand from the start, and giving him "the brumagems" every pace or two, and twice as often if you felt his back getting up (which he used to raise after the manner of a half-starved sow), or at any attempt to get his head down.

After a few ineffectual efforts, in which my steed showed an inclination to differ from me in opinion, we jogged on comfortably for several miles on the edge of prairie and timber, the usual markings of a watercourse. The sun was near mid-day, and still no game was to be seen. No game, in quiet, retired situations like this, is an unhealthy sign. Game are not in the habit of leaving a favourite feeding-ground without reason, and where we were was well known as such. Discouraged at want of success, I dismounted, fastening up Bucephalus, and took my pipe again into confidence. On an old rotten limb of a partially-decayed buttonwood a family of redheaded woodpeckers were busily at work, making the wood echo with the violence of their tapping. Watching the sprightly movements of these active little beauties, I became totally absorbed in their energetic pursuits, when a half snort and uneasy movement on the part of Broomstick caused me to look round, and well I did so, for about forty yards off, leisurely feeding, were about thirty full-grown wild turkeys. My smooth-bore had ball in each barrel, still as I had two or three loads of buck-shot, I determined to substitute the one for the other. Behind a log like a snake I glided to perform the change of missiles, and was about to draw the last fragment of myself out of sight, when the confounded warning of a rattlesnake sounded so close that I involuntarily gave a jump to avoid the threatening danger, when the turkeys took wing, without a chance of a shot at them being afforded, and turkeyless I was compelled to remain; but you may bet that snake never scared anyone afterwards. He was one of the largest and most venomous of his family, being quite five feet long, as yellow as gold along the abdomen, and possessed of sixteen rattles. He belonged to the variety which generally goes by the name of timber-snake, much larger and totally different in colour from the prairie rattlesnake or massasauga, which is always black, and never exceeds eighteen or twenty inches in length.

Having found no game in the timber, I struck out for the open land, and riding several miles I saw two small droves of antelopes. This beautiful animal is very difficult to stalk; but as there appeared to be no other means of getting on intimate terms with them, I hobbled my horse, and taking advantage of all intervening obstacles, managed unseen to get within five hundred yards. Further approach now appeared impossible, and I had almost relinquished the idea, when it struck me that by making a slight detour to leeward I could find a scant shelter from a dip that appeared to lead in the direction of the game. On hands and knees, slowly, I crossed the open, my stomach almost on the ground. The antelopes still continued feeding; so far they had not been alarmed. Twenty yards more would again place me under cover. He who wishes successfully to stalk game must never deem precaution thrown away. On the care with which you pass over an open spot depends often the success of all your labour. With a feeling of gratification I regained shelter, and such shelter as I was able to take the twists and knots out of my legs and arms, with the consciousness that I could do so without imperilling success. A few moments' inspection of the game sufficed. Like a snake in the grass, slowly, but steadily, I made for the back of an unusually high prairie-dog's earth. From the back of it I would be within eighty or a hundred yards of my prey. The antelopes, perfectly ignorant of my presence, were quietly feeding, while occasionally one or two of the youngsters, like young goats, would shake their heads at each other, rear up or stamp with their feet, and make other grotesque threatenings of attack. The prospect of venison was now in the ascendant. I commenced to believe my eggs near enough hatched to count them chickens, when a confounded prairie-dog, who doubtless had been watching all my strategy, uttered his shrill, quick whistle, and took a header into his burrow. This was enough; the antelopes simultaneously closed into a bunch, and with every sense strained, looked eagerly around for the cause of alarm. A closer stalk was impossible, the movement of a mouse could not escape their notice, so springing on one knee, I pulled both triggers almost simultaneously, taking sight for the centre of the ruck. As the smoke lifted, with satisfaction I beheld two victims, one apparently dead, the other making violent efforts to get upon his pins, while the remainder of the drove were scampering across the prairie at such a pace as these animals only are capable of going. As quickly as possible I reloaded my gun, and on advancing to bleed my victims, the wounded buck got his legs under him, and had I not given him the right barrel, a nice clean shot at fifty yards, tumbling him all of a heap, I should have been left with only a solitary specimen.

After bleeding my trophies, I went after Broomstick, who, like all perverse beasts, had fed off at as rapid a pace as possible in exactly the reverse direction to that wanted. Oh, Broomstick, you provoking brute! was ever an unfortunate sportsman so tortured by having to endure the vagaries of so ugly and obstinate a steed! Venting my indignation on his sparsely-covered ribs, and giving him every second stride a reminder that his owner was on his back, I hurried back to my quarry, in the hope of making camp at an early hour, and having a good fire before my comrades returned. Nor was I too soon, for already a coyotte had scented blood, and was about to whet his sharp tusks on the results of my labour. With considerable hoisting I got both antelopes on my nag's rump, lashing them fast with the lariat to the cantle of the saddle, but in this performance I was not successful till I had blindfolded my mount. Swinging myself into the pig-skin, congratulating myself on the success of my stalk, for camp I headed, and already had commenced in imagination to enjoy a hearty meal on some of the tit-bits. Humming possibly the old regimental march, and my thoughts wandering to far-off scenes, I was surprised, on issuing from a dip in the prairie, to see several antelopes feeding undisturbed about a hundred and fifty yards off. Throwing my head forward over the saddletree, in a moment I was on my feet, and hurriedly hobbling my beast, I made a cast to the right to obtain a better leeward position. Prairie-dog earths were numerous, and apparently untenanted, or else the whole population had turned in for their afternoon siesta. These irregularities of the surface afforded an abundance of shelter. A few minutes' crawling, and I was within easy range, when springing to my feet, the game commenced their succession of buck-jumps, which they invariably practise before settling to their regular stride. Pitching my gun to the shoulder, I drew sight upon the leader; over he went; while my second shot, fired too hurriedly, sent its bullet harmlessly ricochetting, its course being marked by a puff of dust where the missile each bound hit the soil. The fall of the leader turned the remainder of the flock, and with the velocity of falcons they rushed past Broomstick; up went his tail and down went his head; half-a-dozen violent struggles, and the hobbling broke. For a moment he stood, then threw his mane recklessly about, turned round and gave his dead load a sniff, and breaking into a succession of buck-jumps, finishing with kicks, divested himself of his burden, and in spite of all I could shout, with the most perfect disregard for consequences, started for home at a pace so unusual and so corky that I vowed if ever I laid leg over him again he should give me a specimen of the same gait for my gratification.

I do not think I ever felt more savage in my life. Two or three times I hesitated whether I would try the effect of a leaden messenger after him; if so long a journey to civilisation had not been before me I believe I should, but finally satisfied myself with the hopes of speedy revenge. After spending half-an-hour in dragging the game together, and possibly as much longer in ruminating over the awkwardness of my position, and the mutability of human and horse affairs, debating the *pros* and *cons* whether to return to camp or remain where I was, to my intense satisfaction I saw one of my comrades coming directly towards me with the now-submissive Broomstick captive, and looking as if any pace faster than that of a funeral procession was entirely beyond his powers of exertion. My friend had spied the truant making straight for camp. After an exciting chase, he had succeeded in capturing him, when by taking the reverse direction from which my nag was seen to come, he happily tumbled across me, much to my relief; for, after all, the little shelter afforded by timber, where you can always have a good fire, is infinitely preferable to a smouldering smudge of buffalo-chips, with the wind playing at hide-and-go-seek round your shirt tails. On reaching the settlements I parted with Broomstick for a fair price. The purchaser was a character; and, judging from the manner he mounted, had never been outside of a horse before. However, he was one of those hawk-featured men that would be about the very last that you would select to trifle with. If he and his horse had not numerous misunderstandings, and if the latter did not get well paid off for the several scurvy tricks he practised on me, I will at once acknowledge that I am no judge of character.

CHAPTER XV.

PINNATED GROUSE.

(Tetrao cupido.)

SCARCELY can I sit to write of this prince of game birds without longing for the delightful weather of September, and the verdant, smooth, undulating prairies of the Western States. The associations connected with this class of shooting are to me delightful, recalling vividly the society of friends and re-unions, the result of sincere friendship. Then it is the advent in America of the shooting-season proper: the gun, which, in many instances, has been shut up in its cell-like case, smothered with tow and grease, has a fresh nativity; the new setters or pointers, reared and broken perhaps far from the owner's eye, have to make their *début*, and not improbably a new sporting suit, fresh from the skilful hands of some reputed clothier, is to have its maiden lustre first dimmed. Every disciple of the chase, if he lives within reach, or has the means wherewith to visit the sacred haunts of these noble fowl, looks forward with as much pleasure to the longed-for period and the anticipated sport as ever did city belle to courtly *fête*, or expectant children to the morrow, which is to announce what the ubiquitous Santa Claus has left for their future amusement. The 12th of August and the 1st of September have for ages been venerated in our tight little island, and been made trysting days as solemnly to be welcomed by the sportsman as has ever been sacred fast by recluse or holiday by gourmand; and although the first legal fixture does not here receive so much attention, the day chosen for each individual's first essay of the season does. The English have long been dubbed a nation of shopkeepers; the Americans, with more justice, might be called a race of traders: for while the former, who are fortunate enough to have the means, invariably tramp down the golden stubble or scatter the purple blooming heather upon the advent morning of shooting, the latter, though possessing the wherewith, have more frequently to wait for days or weeks till press of business or respite in the rush of trade will sanction their absence from the dingy walls or mouldy books of counting-room or office. Again, the acknowledged day in America—the 1st of September—to commence operations on the prairies, is so early in the season that the birds are invariably not full grown, incapable of more than short flights, and the heat is so intense that both Ponto and Juno have had enough quartering and pointing in a couple of hours to satisfy them for that day; so that, if the sportsman has the constitution of a locomotive, with the disregard to heat that is credited to the salamander, if desirous of further replenishing his voluminous skirt pockets, he has to perform not only his own part of the programme, but that of his now half-foundered canines. It has long been a great desire of mine to see one more month granted for these splendid birds to enjoy, uninterrupted, their family cares—a lengthening of the close season which would, not only in many ways be advantageous to both pursuer and pursued, but can have no possible objections, on the other hand, to be urged against it.

The best prairie-chicken shooting I have ever had was in the month of October; and although September had been both wet and boisterous, yet the birds had not packed, and lay well. Day after day I killed from twenty brace upwards, and this in the northern portion of Illinois, with a fourteen-bore, light-made, twenty-six-inch-barrelled gun. I have little hesitation in saying, that if I had had a ten-bore, which I now always use for general shooting in America, my score would have been at least double. As it was I saved nearly every bird, for in the numerous shipments which I made to a wide circle of acquaintances I did not hear of one arriving at its destination unfit for the table. Now, in September, this would have been impossible, though hours had been spent over each packing-case, and the expected hamper contained at starting as much ice and a little more sawdust than game. Some knowing hands profess that by immediately drawing the fowl upon being knocked over, and stuffing a wisp of grass in the cavity, putrefaction will be delayed; but what an agreeable operation to have to perform! Fancy stopping in the middle of a covey, with dogs standing, to perform the functions of the kitchen-maid!—the humanity or refinement of the proceeding, the afterwards loading and handling your handsome breech-loader with your well-daubed hands! or, perhaps in a fit of desperation, caused by the attack of some bloodthirty mosquito giving your nose or forehead the benefit of their friendly intervention! But it is too horrible to think of. All these drawbacks can be warded off or prevented by not shooting till the weather is suitable; or, better still, not permitting shooting till such a date as we have reason to expect a sufficiently cool temperature; making it actionable for game-dealers to expose for sale the temporarily forbidden treasures before the termination of the close season. Gentlemen of America, if you wish to keep game abundant and near home, and to increase and preserve the fine feelings that should imbue the breast of every true sportsman, devote a little attention to this important point.

Like the deer, bear, and sundry varieties of American game, which once were to be found in abundance in almost every section of the country, so was the prairie chicken; but as civilisation and population have increased, in such a ratio their numbers have diminished. In Kentucky, forty years ago, they abounded; it is more than doubtful that this day one can be found in that State. All along the Atlantic seaboard, from Virginia to Maine, they were once to be found; while now, save a scattered few on the scrub plains of Long Island, Martha's Vineyard, and Mount Desert Island, not a single specimen will be seen. The pinnated grouse has abandoned its old haunts, like the Indian, and removes every season farther to the westward, to avoid the society of the pale-faced interloper. Fortunately, all game does not thus dread the stranger's presence, for as civilisation increases so does the partridge, and the familiar call of Bob White will soon entirely supplant the deep, musical, but strange booing of the prairie fowl east of the Mississippi.

To get sport now-a-days, the ultimate western edge of Indiana and the State of Illinois, for the eastern sportsman, are undoubtedly the nearest points; but even after having travelled thus far, if you desire results commensurate with your trouble, rest not near the track of the iron horse, but pursue, to the right or left, your course till you find people who still talk of the cars* as seven-day wonders, and report as a marvel, that one still night, a month ago, Hans or Jacques heard them whistle. When such originals have been found, call a halt, unpack carefully your traps from the waggon and your private store of edibles.

The prairie chickens are very erratic in their habits, and the situations in which they abound one season may be almost entirely deserted the next. It has often puzzled me to account for this strange uncertainty in their choice, and I have thus far failed to satisfy my mind, unless the burning of the grass or inundations, to which the western country is particularly subject, can be accepted as a reason. About two years ago a low prairie close to my dwelling was most amply stocked with prairie fowl, so much so that I used to limit my bag to one dozen and a half, and seldom did it take more than an hour to obtain this number. Last year, on the same land, not one solitary bird was to be found. Now,

* Railroads.

this prairie had not been burnt, although others in the vicinity had undergone the operation. Early in the season, before the young have attained maturity, and ere the cold and boisterous winds of autumn have caused them to pack, the sportsman must indeed be a bad shot who cannot tumble them on nearly each discharge, for they are easy of approach, lying very close, and rising and flying slowly, without making much of that disconcerting disturbance so apparent in the flushing of partridge and of ruffed grouse. Again, the ground in which they are found is open and clear from interruptions, affording an abundance of time for the most precise and formal to take aim ; but after the autumnal equinoctial gales have whistled over the unprotected landscape, and the sharp night frosts have changed the verdant leaves to a vermilion or golden hue, rapid and precise shooting is required, for not only will they rise at long range, but take hard and fair hitting to bring them down, and instead of finding the quarry on the sun-warmed, open, grassy slopes, the dense tall corn will be more frequently selected as their chosen retreat.

Of course, the farther you proceed West, till you reach the ultimate extremities of civilisation, the greater will be your prospects of heavy bags, and more particularly so late in the season, as the population being sparse, and the intrusion of cattle, sheep, and dogs less frequent, the birds still continue comparatively tamer than in the more densely settled quarters. However, it is not convenient for all, nor even would many choose to sacrifice every comfort for the sake of slaughter, and turn a pleasure into a labour and a pursuit of discomfort; for living in a squatter's hut is scarcely, as an old friend used to say, "What it's cracked up to be:" besides, what can you do with the results, a very small portion of which will satisfy your own demands; for my part, give me from eight to ten brace daily, with means of using them, to the most tremendous bags, if they are to be thrown away. Not over two years since, when travelling through a remote and unfrequented section of the State of Illinois, I came across a party of young men who were daily destroying from twenty to thirty couple per gun, and as the season was warm, and the connection with the railroad difficult and uncertain, when asked by the tavern-keeper what they intended doing with their game, they laughingly responded, "Throw it in the hog-pen," and for upwards of a week they continued this dastardly behaviour. Can it then be wondered that game rapidly diminishes, when persons are to be found capable of such disgraceful conduct; the only check that I can see, is the organisation of proper game-laws, prohibiting the birds from pursuit excepting at suitable seasons, the violation of which should be punishable by heavy fines, the whole or greater part to go to the informer.

The pinnated grouse are very capricious in choice of sites on which to place their nests; solitude and vicinity to favourite food or other causes, of which an outsider can know but little, must be accepted as the probable reasons. However, I have generally observed that a preference is shown for those places where the prairie is covered with bunch-grass, particularly if the subsurface is moist, and the neighbourhood not overstocked with cattle. This grouse is easily caused to desert her nest, whether the intrusion be committed by man or beast; on such occasions a new nursery is chosen and a second lot of eggs laid, but if misfortune should deprive her of her brood after the young have left the egg, all idea of raising a second family is laid aside, and the chickless mother joins company with the first similarly-situated unfortunate she may chance to meet. Odd hen-birds, when found by the sportsman, are frequently supposed to be barren, but in nine instances out of ten, I am satisfied that some luckless cur dog, mink, or weasel deserves the onus for the poor bird's chickless lot. Towards the end of March or early in April they commence pairing, the first indication being the booing of the males, which may be heard for upwards of a mile, if the weather is still. This sound, which is very peculiar and melodious, much resembles the lowing of a bull, and has frequently been mistaken for it. The noise is made by the cocks forcing air out of the two inflated air-bags which are to be found on either side of their necks.

Then the large flocks begin to break up and divide into parties of twenty or thirty, each detachment selecting a knoll on which to exhibit their fascinations to the fair sex and select partners. On the first indication of day the males utter their war-cry, and either wait to receive their rivals in love or swiftly wing their way to accept the challenge of some distant gallant. The fiercest battles now ensue;* nor is it only between two, for sometimes a dozen may be observed engaged in the *mêlée*, each fearlessly attacking his nearest neighbour, rising and striking with the wings and feet much after the manner of domestic poultry, when feathers fly and severe and numerous injuries are received, till the weaker, finding their strength inadequate to the trial, reluctantly retire, and some old veteran alone remains,

* Until a late date I believed these battles were a description of tournament, in fact, all for show. However, this is not the case, and numbers of the combatants get severely injured.

exhausted and war-stained, to make selection of his future mate. Often have the birds been found, after these contests, so exhausted that they were scarcely able to rise off the ground or avoid the traveller's feet. And well do the hawks know their enfeebled condition, and are not slow to avail themselves of the advantage and pounce upon the unfortunate conquerors, who, but for their prowess and now-exhausted condition, could easily have beaten off the relentless destroyer. As soon as the victor has made his choice he retires. The same scenes are again and again enacted till all are mated.

Like the turkey-cock and domestic pigeon, when making love they ruffle their feathers, drop their wings and tails, and strut about with more pomposity than ever did city beau.

The nest, which is generally placed upon the top of a hillock among the long grass, in shape is irregular, but on examination it will be found carefully constructed of leaves and interwoven grasses. The eggs, which seldom exceed twelve, are a trifle smaller than those of the domestic fowl, and are of a dull, yellowish colour, much resembling those of the ruffed grouse. In eighteen or nineteen days they are hatched, and the chicks leave their nest immediately afterwards. From this period the female is deserted by her mate, and until severe weather causes them to pack, the old males and females are not found again together.

In crossing the prairie, I have often come across the hen engaged with the charge of her diminutive family, and the anxiety and courage she will display if suddenly surprised, is truly amusing. But the young are seldom in danger from man, for their powers of concealment are wonderful, and unless aided by a dog, it is impossible for a human being to find their retreat. On several occasions I have jumped off my shooting-pony, confident of success, but never succeeded in their capture, unless on such occasions as one of my setters was in company.

By the first week in August they are capable of short flights, when they do not much exceed our partridge in size, and if shot thus early, which is too frequently the case, it is difficult to imagine more delicious food; but they will not bear keeping, and sooner taint than any other game-bird I am acquainted with. In October they have attained full strength of wing, becoming more difficult of approach daily till severe weather has caused them to pack, when they will seldom lie, either to dog or gun, unless when feeding in tall corn or dusting themselves at mid-day if there should chance to be a strong sun.

Although the pinnated grouse seldom leave the open

country, yet if winter be excessively severe they will frequent the edges of the timber, roosting on the tallest trees, more particularly girdlings or those destitute of small limbs. Under such circumstances they are exceedingly wild, and the most successful deer or turkey-hunter may practise all his cunning and most cautious methods of approach with signal failure in getting even within rifle range; however, in a snow-storm, by putting white clothes on, or a night-gown over your attire and tying a towel around your head, at feeding-time, when they are seated on the fences or corn-stacks, you can easily get within ten or fifteen yards of them.

When flushed they invariably utter several separate clucks, but after they have succeeded in placing a safe distance between themselves and the intruder they continue their course in silence; nor if when on the wing they should chance to fly over a sportsman do they repeat their note of alarm.

Their favourite food is buckwheat, corn, oats, wheat, and grass-seed, the buds of fruit trees and the seed of the sumach.

Their size is eighteen inches long by twenty-seven inches across the wings; bill short, stout and curved, with the upper mandible considerably overlapping the lower; legs feathered to the ankle; feet of ordinary size;

toes covered above with numerous small scales; hind toes very short; claws moderately long, curved and concave beneath; feathers compact, those of the head and neck long and flexible, with a continuation tapering to a crest on back of head; on either side a tuft of fine long hackles, covering a bare portion, which is orange coloured in the males and dull brown in the females; the wings short and much rounded; pin feathers hard and short; tail short and fan-like, composed of eighteen broad feathers; bill dusky; iris yellow; toes dull yellow; claws bluish; the neck and upper portion of back dark brown, mixed with grey, getting lighter beneath; tail dirty brown, tipped with white, except the middle feathers, which are mottled with a deep brown; and a dark line from mandible to eye, thence back to neck, and a beautiful patch of soft slate-coloured feathers under each wing, invaluable to the fly-tier,— is a correct description of their appearance.

CHAPTER XVI.

TROUT* FISHING IN MAINE.

As the seasons roll past in rapid succession, and each year appears to flit by with more velocity than its predecessor, the same pleasures, the same sports recur to our memory, always with the appetite more sharpened for their enjoyment by the lapse of the close season, in which the true sportsman would not enjoy his favourite pastime, even if law and weather were not both adverse. Age, if not accompanied by infirmity, in few instances reduces the enjoyment of field-sports, if they were in our youth our all-absorbing passion. A few pleasant spring-like days have their effect upon the angler; he that is skilled in flies and rods,—he that well knows the resorts of the speckled beauties of the brook, their habits, and their devices to

* (*Salmo fontinalis.*) Live specimens of these fish, which I procured last winter in America, may now be seen alive at Mr. Buckland's Museum of Economic Fish Culture, Royal Horticultural Gardens, South Kensington.

escape the landing-net, after the insidious, treacherous hook has pierced their mouth,—commences living in anticipation, and, doubtless with faithful and well-tried friends, plans numerous and stolen visits to favourite streams or well-stocked rivers.

Rods, lines, flies, and reels, which have for months rested in dusty closet or well-secured packing-case, again see the light of day and undergo careful scrutiny, that neither break nor flaw may be unrepaired; rings which were lost the previous season are now replaced; frayed wrappings of silk have been stopped, a drop or two of oil has been donated to the sonorous reel, and, doubtless, the moths have had sundry imprecations hurled at them for wholesale destruction of gaudy feathers, which have cost many a pound, or sundry hours of labour to procure, and whose deficiency has got to be replaced before the outfit can be deemed perfect. Of all field sports, there is none that requires more particular attention to all the many details; every portion must be kept in perfect repair, for the probability is, that the very first time you are caught wanting you will have reason to rue it for the balance of the season. Strange as it may appear, we have invariably found it so. If we were scant of tackle, or our outfit had become injured, and unreliable, we were certain to hook a heavy fish, such a one as required the utmost skill and attention under favourable circumstances to master. Of course, as might be expected, the wreck was completed by a break, and the foe made good his escape. However, it invariably happens that the angler considers those that escape much larger than any that have succumbed. A day or two since, having some business in that portion of the town where many of the *élite* of the disciples of dear old Izaak congregate, I came across two whose prowess and skill had been well tried by long experience, and whose success as anglers is probably second to no others. After the usual greetings, the *sine qua non*, the *ne plus ultra* of their pleasures were broached, and the prospects discussed. May we say that it was with feelings almost akin to selfishness that we listened to the numerous delightful distant visits arranged, where well-stocked murmuring brooks or rapid rivers pursue their erratic and picturesque course to the ocean, far, far away from the busy haunts of man, where the wild duck and deer rear their harmless young, and where the lordly, silver-sheened salmon leaps in sportive plunge over the foaming crest of the headlong rapid? But no such trip is in store for us. Pens, ink, and paper have to be our companions, and the monotonous and well-known walls of a city do duty for a rural landscape.

Of all the localities where trout fishing can be enjoyed in perfection, the State of Maine in North America, in our opinion, is the most deserving of notice, for not only can the fisherman here capture immense numbers, but occasionally a giant, whose efforts for liberty will imbue the angler with a due appreciation of the power and perseverance of the monarch of the brook. The scenery also in this State is truly magnificent, being as diversified by wood, mountain and water, and that in such close proximity and rapid succession as must please the taste of the most fastidious *connoisseur*. Supposing that the fisherman, say about the middle of May, should choose to visit these haunts, it may be a saving of considerable trouble to know the most convenient method of reaching the homes of the speckled beauties. We are aware that a Railroad Guide is always one of the most intricate and mysterious books to the uninitiated, and would, therefore, in the cause of humanity, save you the unsatisfactory task of hunting over Appleton's, (the Bradshaw of America), or others of these far from lucid works, for the requisite information. Moreover, it is well for a fisherman to arrive at his destination in an amiable frame of mind, and at peace with all men, which we consider morally impossible if he fail to make connections in the railroads, or is bullied by officious conductors, or left shivering in some out-of-the-way situation where nought can be done but smoke and court Somnus in a railroad wrapper. To avoid all these troubles, and, probably, a great many more, if New York be your starting-place, take steamboat thence to Portland,—a delightful short cruise of from thirty to thirty-six hours,—and if you should experience bad weather, especially if it results in seasickness, the ulterior effects will be beneficial, *terra firma* will be more appreciated, and your appetite stimulated to an unusual extent. Besides, the scenery, in those places where land is visible, is pretty, while fleets of fishing and trading crafts will be constantly in sight. The steam-vessels on this route are very comfortable and sea-worthy, and under the command of most able officers.

Having arrived at Portland, and enjoyed a good meal and rest at one of the numerous hotels, the terminus of the Grand Trunk Railroad will have to be reached, where you will procure your ticket for Bethel, Oxford County. The scenery through which you will now rush, dragged by the iron horse, is magnificent, alike suited to the taste of artist or sportsman; but one thing is certain to cause a regret, viz., that the numerous beautiful rivers and brooks that so frequently will be seen or traversed, are now destitute of fish,—at least so I was informed, although I could not learn the reason. Visions of mill dams, without fish-ways, and tons of sawdust floating in islands, hovered before me, and, probably, whispered a true cause of the destruction of the thousands of fish which doubtlessly swarmed here before *genus homo*, with his devices and march of improvement, had defiled these formerly pure, pellucid brooks. Bethel, where you leave the train, will be found a model village, which, for cleanliness and neatness, it would be impossible to surpass. As you progress along the principal thoroughfare, the pretty dwellings, overshadowed by handsome shade trees, remind you of some of Longfellow's beau ideal New England homes. The hotel, also, is very comfortable, and Mr. Lovejoy, the proprietor, can give good information and instruction as to your future proceedings. He also will supply you with a conveyance to take you to Upton, distant about twenty-seven miles, over a road far from good; but if the weather be fine, you will be so delighted with the beautiful panoramas of wild and magnificent scenery that time will slip by rapidly, and ruts and jolts will be totally forgotten. For the first five or six miles of your drive you pass along the margin of the grand Androscogan River, exhibiting a succession of pools and rapids, so eminently suited for retreats for salmon, that you cannot fail to regret that these noble fish are debarred from visiting this choice water. A few miles farther your course winds by a beautiful mountain brook well stocked with trout, and in which a good basket can always be taken. We will now suppose you have reached the half-way house, a pretty little road-side tavern, where the horses are baited, and the traveller, if he chooses—we would strongly advise you not to fail to—may make the acquaintance of mine host, a worthy man with a wonderful fund of information on various interesting subjects. The allotted half-hour having expired, and the inner man been refreshed, forward is again the word, and more beautiful becomes the scenery. Wild, irregular hills, with bases densely covered with timber, but stony and irregular towards their summit, frown over your head; precipices, cliffs, and yawning chasms alternately vary the prospect, throwing, for grandeur, the choicest wilds of Scotland in the shade. Only an able poet, with a romantic turn of mind, is wanted to immortalise by soul-stirring lays these stupendous mountain fastnesses, accessible alone to the wild denizens of the forest, or to him who is gifted with the nerve, steady foot, and reliable eye of the chamois hunter of the Alps.

Having at length reached the upper portion of the village of Upton, an entire change comes over the landscape; far beneath your feet, lies nestled, in all the splendour of luxuriant timber, with irregular and changing outline, the lovely sheet of water, Umbagog, thickly studded with innumerable islands of every form, size, and outline. On first beholding this scene, Loch Lomond was vividly recalled to mind, and the more frequently we beheld this picture, the stronger was the impression of the striking similarity. Again, this lake will have additional charms to the sportsman, for here trout abound in immense numbers. But supposing you started from Bethel after breakfast, the sun must now be near dipping the horizon, when you have reached thus far, so that you had better hurry forward and gain the hospitable roof-tree of Mr. Simeon Frost, the hotel proprietor, ere night envelopes the earth with her sombre mantle of darkness.

Being met on the porch by the honest, straightforward Simeon, you may safely resign yourself to his care, which would be dangerous in this *locale* in many other hands, as some of the hosts are peculiar in their belief, and strongly adhere to a sinister interpretation of the words, "I was a stranger and ye took me in." But once marshalled under the banner of Mr. Frost, you will be safe from their philanthropic designs; and further, you will be well fed and housed. If you be an epicure, fail not to ask for a *bonne bouche*—which we relished among these pine-clad hills—viz., trout stewed in cream. The white-bait of the Londoner, the canvas-back duck of Delmonico's, and the green turtle-steak of the City Fathers, are all thrown in the shade by this delicious dish. You have but to scent it in future to make your mouth water, and visions of epicurean feasts float before your eyes. Now, if you will only place yourself in my hands—and well I know the smooth water and rocky shoals, the pleasures and disappointments that beset the stranger in this beautiful but inhospitable region—I will keep your feet free from pitfalls, and your purse safe from too-frequent incursions. Having eaten your evening meal, and retired to your room, send for your host, and learn from him all particulars necessary to guide your future steps. Wherever you go you will catch fish; sometimes the fishing at Errol[*] is so good as to well deserve a visit ere you go up to the dam where the Androscogan River leaves Lower Richardson Lake. Supposing the season to be the end of May—the time we should advise to be selected for your visit—delightful brook-fishing may be obtained beneath the dam in the Little Cambridge River, which flows within fifty yards of the hotel. Many and many a morning and evening I have taken here three or four dozen beauties, some of them over a pound, and all game to the last. I know no

[*] A village a few miles distant from Upton.

river better suited for the increase of trout, and doubtless at the present time it would swarm with thousands all along its course, but that some selfish being projected and erected a dam about twenty feet high, to collect water to drive a mill; and worse, had the inhumanity not even to leave a fish-way; consequently, Izaak Walton's disciples have to walk many a wearisome mile up this brook before fish can again be found abundant, and then they are so poor and badly fed that they are almost unfit for the table. Now, the difference between those beneath the dam and those above, is doubtlessly caused by the unfortunate denizens of the upper water being prevented from making their annual visits to Lake Umbagog to recruit, or enjoy the cool retreats afforded in its deep waters, at that portion of the season when the summer sun pours down its refulgent, heated rays upon the unprotected water. Persons who resided in this locality years ago, informed me that before this impediment on the Cambridge was made, trout swarmed all the way up to the source in ten times the quantity they do now. But why grumble or find fault in this particular instance? Are such shameful structures not to be found in every section of this and my own land, a glaring example of want of forethought, or selfishness, or worse? But, thank goodness, such abuses in America are about to be stopped;

State legislation has taken the matter in hand, and is determined to enforce such severe penalties, that we hope, ere long, to see the temporarily-deserted retreats of the spotted, brilliant-hued trout again teeming with their numbers, and the placid, sheltered pools, now still and tenantless, boiling with their breaks and rises, as they either roll over in sport, or rush headlong to the surface after the dainty and fragile ephemera.

A lady, who formed one of our party, frequently of an evening, without moving from the bridge, took a dozen fish in an hour or so, plainly proving that even the uninitiated can here be successful, for Madame previously had never seen a trout captured in her life. The flies which we should recommend for this stream are about the same in size as those in use on Scotch and Irish rivers, and of the same colouring, black and red hackles being preferable. We also found a fly constructed as follows most killing: wings from the tail of the ruffed grouse, with a few strands of scarlet ibis, brown cock's hackle under wings, body of ground hog's fur, plucked off the stomach, with a couple of strands of guinea-fowl feather for tail. If the water should have been discoloured with rain, substitute a little of the golden-pheasant topknot for the termination, instead of the guinea-fowl. By coming here early in the season, as above advised, you will moreover escape the attacks of those confounded pests, the black flies, which generally make their appearance the second week of June, when woe betide you; for if you are compelled to submit to their persecutions, your tortures from the results might turn your hair grey in a night, or drive you crazy for the remainder of life. No one can sympathise with the unfortunate Egyptians so well as he who has visited the Maine fishing-regions in the fly season; getting rid of the Israelites, if they took the plague with them, was under any circumstances most desirable.

Before leaving Upton for the Wilds, as by this name your future resting-places may well be called, we would revert to the practice of throwing sawdust that comes from mills into the water. Now, although some may not be aware of it, there is nothing more destructive to trout and salmon than these minute particles of timber. The fish, as they rest head up stream, imbibe them into their mouths, whence they pass into the gills and stomach, ultimately causing disease and death. When this is known to be the case, would it not be well to insist that this *débris* should otherwise be disposed of, which may, without much labour or inconvenience, be accomplished by fire, after transporting it to a suitable distance. Hendrick Hudson, the first explorer of the magnificent river which bears his name in America, speaks of that river as swarming with salmon; but where are they now? Gone, never to return, unless repopulated by artificial means; in fact, expelled by dams and sawdust, and such like accompaniments of the human race. As with the Hudson, so it would be everywhere, if preventive measures were not adopted to stop these abuses, so glaring and unjustifiable, that every well-thinking man can scarce fail to anathematise the short-sighted policy that has formerly marked the advance of civilisation. But it is not only fish in America; game has also thus ruthlessly been dealt with, till forests and farms cease to re-echo the musical, plaintive notes of the partridge, or the sonorous, drumming call of the ruffed grouse. For our part, the most picturesque walk, the most delightful rural drive, if not graced with the presence or note of the feathered warblers, the cooing of the dove, or the flight of birds, loses half its fascinations, half its enchantments, and consequently half the pleasures it would otherwise afford.

Supposing that you have passed a few days at Upton, and enjoyed, with that relish which is so natural to a sportsman, the manifold pleasures of a country excursion, we should advise your now leaving civilisation and revelling in the solitude of the pathless wood, where man seldom intrudes and nature remains undefiled or deformed except by the assassin hand of the axeman. If you be a good pedestrian, we would recommend your feet as the most enjoyable and natural method of gaining the portage where the upper Androscogan has to be crossed; but as you may not be experienced in woodcraft, and all the sciences that teach the solitary hunter to surely follow a blazed path, procure the services of Collins, an agreeable and obliging man, to perform the duty of guide; and if he still possesses his noble dog, the jaunt might possibly be diversified by the treeing of a bear, for Mr. Bruin here roams at large, undisputed master of a gigantic demesne. At the same time, care must be taken to ascertain that a boat is available to transport you across the river, for thus early in the season the water will be found too high and too cold for fording or swimming.

But if previous confinement and sedentary habits have relaxed the muscles and made the feet tender, get Mr. Frost to negotiate for the services of the steamboat,* taking care that a direct understanding as to charge is made before embarking. In fact, go not to the dam; do nothing till you are certain what will be the cost; for once you are caught sleeping, if away

---

* By what other name to desigate this extraordinary piece of mechanism I know not, but be advised while on board always to keep the wood bunkers between you and the boiler.

from Mr. Frost's protecting influence, you may, on awakening, find your molars gone, or your strength, if it consists in the length of your purse. To be forewarned is to be forearmed, and now if you fall into the snare, blame not the writer.

The voyage by water, distance fourteen or fifteen miles, is charming; after leaving the place of embarkation you proceed about two miles down the Cambridge, which is here dead and sluggish,* till you reach the entrance to Lake Umbagog, when your vessel's prow is pointed for distant hills fringed with giant timber. On either side, islands after islands dot the bosom of the water, while verdant mountains and primeval forests stretch far, far beyond the limits allotted to vision. The two or three hours which are taken to cross the lake will flit by rapidly, if you have appreciation of what is sublime, of what Nature in her grand conceptions formed, and the impressions indented on the tablets of your memory will doubtlessly be permanent. It matters not how sceptical and unbelieving some may be, place them where the giant works of the Creator are visible, and how insignificant for ever after must they view the puny efforts and constructions of their fellow-beings, and cease to disbelieve that there is One above omnipotent and all-powerful!

Fail not, on reaching the centre of the lake, to face

* Once a favourite haunt for moose.

about and look for the White Mountains,* and if the day is clear, ample will be your recompense, for, towering high above all other contestants, they frown gloriously over the landscape, softened into a dreamy reality by distance, and furrowed on their summits by lines of virgin snow, reflecting a thousand brilliant prismatic colourings. But the irrevocable pace of time glides on, and pleasure flits with rapid stride. Our primitive boat now appears to head direct on shore, and so we advance till, when within a few yards of the rocks, the helm is put hard down, and we quickly turn to the left and enter the Androscogan, up whose waters a most charming vista is beheld, the drooping limbs of the trees on either side playfully kissing the rippling stream, and the irregularly formed rocks splitting the water, and, diverting its course in tangent lines, making many a miniature whirlpool or gurgling eddy, the haunt and breeding-place of innumerable trout. If the river is sufficiently high you will be able to proceed, without leaving the steamboat, as far as the commencement of the portage; but, should it be otherwise, your baggage and self will require to be transferred to boats, to be propelled up stream by pole and paddle in the skilful hands of some of the proficient backwoodsmen.

* Mount Washington is six thousand feet high.

The trip up the river is worthy all the distance you have travelled. The view is ever changing and ever beautiful: now you float over some still, dark pool; next, with laborious and slow progress, ascend some seething rapid; one time the centre of the stream only is navigable, the next moment the brush and branches on the margin grate against your boat's gunwale. A solemn stillness reigns around, only broken by the murmuring of the water, the occasional shrill cry of the fish hawk, or the laborious, incessant hammering of the industrious woodpecker. Again, as you advance, many a wild duck or merganser, on rapid wing, will whistle past, or flutter over the rippling stream, followed by a numerous, inoffensive brood, perhaps but the other day divested of the egg-shell, yet, thus early, proficient in aquatic exercise—all adding peace to the scene and suitable figures for foreground to the picture.

From this point, where you leave the boats, a portage of four miles occurs, which has to be traversed on foot; however, the walking is not bad, although too rough for driving. The path is well defined and erratic, one moment pointing direct for the impenetrable woods, the next following the margin of the river. Some persons have christened this portion of the Androscogan "Mad River," a name far from inappropriate, as for more than a mile it is one succession of grand rapids and miniature cascades, boiling, surging, and rushing for the placid bosom of Lake Umbagog. Good fly-fishing can be obtained at low water all along this portion close to the margin, where the water forms many miniature eddies, but woe betide your tackle if you should chance to hook a heavy fish, whose gallant spirit dictates a rush for the turbid centre stream! no rod or line on earth could possibly hold, and the shores are too rough for the angler to follow downwards.

It will be well to have a gun with you in taking the tramp across this portage. The first time we traversed it we saw a young bear, and the last time one of our party came in such close contact with an old lady bruin as to be frightened almost to death, if it is admissible to judge from his appearance rather than from his description.

Having progressed a little over half the distance, a pretty fishing-shanty, the property of a Bostonian, most opportunely offers itself as a resting-place, while the panorama from its porch fairly earns the eulogy of sublimity. Above, below, and in front seethes the precipitous river, white with foam, while in the distance the placid surface of a miniature lake, unpoetically dubbed "the Pond," recalls to memory the stories of our childhood, in which naiads and nymphs, with the enchanting Lurline for their sovereign, prominently figure.

The Pond, at some seasons, affords splendid sport, especially at the entrance and exit of the river, which flows through it, but it cannot be fished except from a boat, which can be brought down, if desired, from the dam above,—no easy task to be performed, but frequently accomplished by the expert lumbermen, who appear equally at home in handling the axe or shooting rapids in their flat-bottomed punts.

Having rested sufficiently to recruit, and probably imbibed a small glass of something stimulating, diluted with water that trickles from a neighbouring spring— which is always cold as ice however warm the weather may be—as scarcely more than a couple of miles are before us, we may just as well hurry on. The walk now leaves the river and becomes much more hilly and enclosed; one time crossing a deep boggy ravine, the next, threading its erratic course along the summit of some stony hill-side. The timber here is very beautiful, much superior to what we have formerly met, and the graceful, silver birch prevails—a tree than which no prettier or more beautiful exists. Although the road, in some places, must be quite half a mile from the water, still the deep rumbling of the numerous rapids is distinctly audible—the neighbouring portion of the Androscogan River being wild and broken in the extreme.

We have scarcely ever threaded this part of our journey without seeing ruffed grouse, and frequently Canada grouse, one of the most beautiful of the indigenous birds, and resembling more closely than any of the American family the red grouse of Scotland; the deep scarlet iris, the rich, dark chestnut colouring of both are similar; but they are totally opposed to one another in habits of life, the one preferring the open, heather-covered mountain slopes—wild as a hawk, unless when engaged with family cares—the other, thoughtless and careless of danger, and never seen away from the densest retreats of the woods. So tame are the Canada grouse that, during my residence in Maine, I knew one of the hotel proprietor's sons to catch an old cock-bird, by slipping a noose, attached to the end of a stick, over its head. But our promenade is near an end. The woods appear less dense as we advance, and soon the flag, that floats over the shanty which is to be our future dormitory, appears in view, with the placid waters of Richardson Lake close by, while numerous irregular hills, all clothed with pine timber to the summit, form the background.

Generally this beautiful lake is smooth as glass, without a ripple, excepting what may be caused by the break of fish, or sudden appearance or descent of the great northern diver, whose wild weird notes have not unfrequently startled the uninitiated, brought a cold shiver to their system, or vividly recalled stories of ghosts, sprites, panthers, and wild cats. You are at last fairly in the wilds, miles from man's habitation—if you except a couple of fishing shanties only occupied a few weeks yearly. You may strain your eyes up and down, no snow-white, smiling cottage will greet your vision. This country is the same still as in the days when the red man knew no superior, and owned every inch of soil from the Atlantic to the Pacific, save it be that the cruel axe of the lumberman has culled out the choicest giant monarchs of the forest. But having done a pretty good day's walking, we may as well lay up for an hour or so, before making our *début* on the Androscogan; moreover, the trout in the middle of the day do not rise so freely, and a couple of hours' work in the evening, if the weather is propitious, will afford as many fish and as much sport as the most exacting can possibly desire.

In the spring the best fishing is to be obtained underneath the dam—which is built across the river a few hundred yards below where it debouches from the lake, and formed for the purpose of gathering a good head of water to assist in shooting the lumbermen's logs. In autumn, however, it is the reverse, for above the dam the greatest numbers and the heaviest fish are found. Why trout should, at the various seasons, select different resorts, is still a matter of surmise; our opinion is, that in summer all that are able leave the river and betake themselves to the locality of the springs in the bottom of the lake, or lie down in such deep water as has not been rendered tepid by the rays of the sun; but as the season advances, and becomes proportionably cool, the fish retake themselves to the streams, either for the purpose of spawning, or because the rapid water is a more suitable residence during the severity of a northern winter. This migration, if such it may be called, has a great resemblance to the movements of salmon, except that the latter have the choice of the ocean instead of the land-locked lakes. From the above, our readers will see that midsummer is not the season to select for a visit to this picturesque neighbourhood, even supposing that the flies and mosquitoes were less numerous; but even if the sport was then to be enjoyed in perfection, the assaults of the insatiable pests would render the most fascinating pleasure of fly-fishing a perfect labour.

Turning from the house, a foot-path, sufficiently clear to permit you to carry your rod ready for work, leads off to the right, and soon you reach the river, tumbling with a headlong, impetuous rush through several flood-gates and a shoot.* The river above and below the fall is lovely, yet almost the opposite in effect. Looking towards the lake the water is placid and calm, with islands and bays, covered or sheltered with trees, reposing in quiet peace, while beneath the fall, from the effects of the descent, a broad course of white foam-water rushing with headlong speed, first striking one margin, then ricochetting towards the other,—now divided by abrupt rocks of irregular outline, or swaying round in real whirlpools,—descends on its uncontrollable route. The best stand to fish from, for those who object to wet feet, is a rock about the size of a waggon, thirty or forty yards beneath the falls, on the right-hand side. From this place a person may work for hours with constant success. However, if the visitor be of an adventurous disposition and fears not to wade, the opposite shore is well worthy of attention; but as the bottom is extremely rough and irregular, and in some parts the current very strong, care must be taken not to make a false step or stumble, as fatal results might be the consequence. I should advise the constant use of the handle of your landing net to feel and guide your steps, on no account permitting the excitement of hooking a large fish to make you lose your head.

* A smooth incline, down which the logs are floated.

A couple of hundred yards beneath the dam is a splendid pool, difficult to fish and difficult of access, but your perseverance will be amply rewarded. Scarcely in the memory of a long fishing career have we ever enjoyed such a couple of hours' sport as fell to our luck the first time we wetted a line upon its well-stocked surface. On the first cast not one but half a dozen of the spotted beauties rushed to the surface, so that we were ultimately compelled to reduce the number of flies we were using to a solitary specimen. For two hours we confined ourselves to this pool, with the simple change of altering situation or cast, and even then only desisted, not from want of fish, but for fear the constant strain would wear out the rod. On this occasion the results were nearly four dozen, and none under half a pound, many reaching as high as three and even three and a half. The guide, whom I have previously mentioned, was my companion, and most satisfactorily he did his work, although on many occasions he was compelled to wade up to his middle; in fact, I never met a more obliging person, or one more fearless in entering water, or better skilled in handling a landing net.

The flies I would advise for use are the same in size as those generally employed for sea-trout fishing, but less gaudy. However, if the water should be very clear and low, it would be well to use smaller. On every occasion not more than two flies should be employed at the same time, as in this portion of the Androscogan fish are abundant and sometimes very large, and you may chance to impale a couple of gentlemen that will give you more to do than desirable. Having spent as much time here as you feel inclined, I would advise your proceeding to the upper dam, fifteen miles farther on. The sail is pretty and picturesque, particularly through the passage denominated the Narrows, which connects upper and lower Richardson Lakes. If adverse winds do not oppose your progress, five or six hours will be sufficient to transport you to your destination; but if they should set in, your patience will be severely tried, and a temporary encampment for the night, in some well-sheltered valley, be found preferable to buffeting on the lake.

During our sojourn a steamboat was spoken of to ply between these two points, for the better accommodation of visitors; of course, if it is built, much time will be saved and considerable inconvenience. The table and accommodation at the Upper Dam are very good, considering its isolated position; moreover, the employés are civil and attentive—which cannot be said for those at the lower establishment.

Charges are not nearly so exorbitant here as at the Lower Dam, although all the provisions supplied by the proprietor have to be transported a greater distance.

The same flies as used before will here be found to answer equally well, and the weight of the fish to range higher. During my stay, I heard of a Bostonian killing two trout at one time, each weighing nearly seven pounds, but such a performance as this is rare; in truth such an essay should form an era in the lifetime of any of the disciples of Izaak Walton.*

* These lakes are known by the extraordinary Indian names of Moonluckmaguntic and Mollechunkamunk.

CHAPTER XVII.

INSTRUCTIONS FOR SPORTSMEN.

THERE are no classes of society who are more apt to be doubted in their assertions than travellers and sportsmen. I will not deny that they are occasionally given to exaggeration, but frequently the excitement under which they may have laboured, at the period of beholding what is strange and novel, causes them unwittingly themselves to be deceived.

When Gordon Cumming's narrative of sporting events first made its appearance, the majority of readers were inclined to doubt the veracity of his statements, more particularly in reference to the countless herds of wild animals that could be seen frequently in a day's ride. Poor Bruce, one of the greatest of African explorers, after years of toil and research spent in his country's service, enduring fatigue, hunger, and thirst, had the mortification to find himself entirely disbelieved on his return to his native land, and not till lately has proper credit been given to this patriotic man, years after he has mouldered to dust, because not till lately did research confirm the truth of all he had stated. Not caring whether or not I am believed, for the ignorant are ever the most sceptical, I state that more buffalo will be sometimes seen in a day's ride over the gigantic western table-lands of America than ever spectator beheld of domestic cattle in the best adapted region for growing stock.

Kind reader, fancy yourself transported from the busy haunts of man, far, far beyond the turbid waters of the giant Mississippi, to the rolling uplands that border the vertebrate chain of mountains which longitudinally intersects the western continent: the season, spring of the year, when tender, succulent grasses commence to sprout, and if you have the fortune to strike the chosen route selected by these superb and matchless animals, you will behold a migration, which for numbers appears to equal the dense flights of the wild pigeon or innumerable phalanxes of duck pursuing their biannual journey to and from the sterile north. And for grandeur of effect, all other sights fall far short of this to the sportsman's eye, the surface of the ground being frequently obscured, and nought but a dense, uncountable surging mass of dark, tawny hides, whose tramping and lowing can be heard for miles, offering itself to view.

At one period the buffalo was to be found almost all over the American continent, from the St. Lawrence to Florida, and from the Atlantic to the Pacific; but cultivation and emigration have done here their usual havoc, and not a single specimen can now be found in many localities where fifty years ago they swarmed; and if we look into futurity, say fifty years hence, it is more than probable that but few of these lordly animals will exist. Like the poor red man, their days are numbered, and to future generations nought will remain but the reminiscence or literary mention of these races. This animal forms the principal resource of the Indian—his food, his covering, and his amusement; it is even the constant topic of his conversation, and the two, that are thus closely associated, are doubtless destined to make their final exit from the world about the same date.

While these animals exist in numbers, and travelling is so easily accomplished, it is surprising that more of our gentlemen do not visit their resorts, to enjoy with uninterrupted freedom a sport which is at the same time exciting and healthful; true, to be a proficient requires many qualities, such as a firm seat on horseback, a quick eye and ready hand, decision and capacity to act on an emergency, with a constitution and physique capable of bearing fatigue and hardship. But still, although you lack some of the above, you may have ample sport, a thousand times to repay you for both outlay and loss of time; for few ever return whose health has not been benefited by the trip; the pure unadulterated air and wholesome primitive diet suffusing the cheek with the ruddy glow of health, and imparting an energy and strength only too often wanting in those whose callings constantly incarcerate them in over-populated cities.

For those contemplating such an excursion the experiences of one who has trod the path are not without value, so that I will endeavour to impart my knowledge. First and foremost, take as little baggage as it is possible to do with; let your horse or horses be as good and well bred as you can procure,—mules being preferable to carry baggage,—and your ammunition and arms of the best quality, always taking care of the latter yourself, and never leaving camp without them; for remember, you are in a country where scalps are at a premium and life deemed of little value, skulking hostile redskins only kept civil through intimidation, and rascally whites (even more to be dreaded) by knowing that the odds are against them if they should attempt any liberties.

Why I prefer thoroughbred horses, or those nearly

so, is that speed is one of the great desiderata required; and again, they are generally pleasanter in their paces and cleverer on their feet. Moreover, I am inclined to believe they can stand hardship and even work better than half-bred brutes;* at the same time I would particularly caution you against a headstrong, nervous devil, who gallops with his head in the air as if he was star-gazing, or one whose mouth is so hard that it requires constant exertion to keep him under control. for out of such you can never expect to make a good buffalo-runner. Small horses I also prefer to big ones; it may only be a fancy. but I always think that they are more generally well made and are tougher. Few nags at first will be got to range alongside your quarry, but after a few essays, if practised judiciously, this objection will be overcome. For shooting buffalo when running them, as the range is only a few feet, a large-bored breech-loading pistol will be found the most convenient, as it can be rapidly loaded by placing the stock under your left thigh and between it and the flap of the saddle, and does not require capping, an operation which on horseback can scarcely be performed without using both hands; and where the riding is rough and irre-

* During the Crimean campaign I frequently remarked how much better the well-bred horses stood the hardships than those of common lineage.

gular, particularly if your horse is blown, relinquishing the hold of your nag's head will not unfrequently seriously incommode your animal, and sometimes cause both him and the rider abruptly to become acquainted with the surface of the soil.

A good rifle and shot-gun will also find abundant work, for besides the grand buffalo, abundance of other game will be found, such as deer, antelope, bear, and wild fowl, all welcome additions to the fare of the hungry hunter. In selecting a rifle for this purpose it should not be small in the bore, an error that too many make, originating doubtlessly from the pioneers and trappers who first visited these distant regions being compelled to use such weapons, from the saving of ammunition, and the comparatively trifling injury a small bullet would do to the hide. Doubtless, a small bullet properly placed will do all that is necessary, but should your projectile deviate the slightest to the right or left, you may have the satisfaction of seeing your game go off for parts unknown, or have the felicity of being placed in juxtaposition with a wounded, dangerous customer; whereas, if the ball had been a large one, the paralysation that would have resulted to the animal's system from the concussion, and the hæmorrhage that would ensue from the size of the wound, would at once incapacitate the stricken from further exertion. I am aware that my ideas on the above point will have many adversaries, more particularly among Americans, but I feel certain, after years of experience, that I am right, and that continued adherence to the old theory of using small bores is but the result of custom and obstinacy, examples of which we can see every day in the tenacity with which the old muzzle-loader was upheld in the army, or still more so, in the years that elapsed before sportsmen could be induced to resign the antiquated flint-gun for the more modern percussion.

An addition to a hunting *cortége*, which may be difficult to obtain, but worthy of any amount of trouble, for they will afford you more real sport than anything I am aware of, is, a couple or more large rough greyhounds, such as are known familiarly as the Scotch deer-hounds; but as this breed is scarce, an admirable substitute can be obtained by the following cross,—three-quarters greyhound and one-quarter mastiff or foxhound, the former preferable. They are the only dogs that can catch and kill a wolf, and many is the pleasant hour you may enjoy pursuing these prowlers. Deer, when you can get them in the open, will be easily overtaken by these dogs; they will also be found no small protection for your camp at night, for all the greyhound family are gifted with remarkably quick sight and hearing, and when crossed, as above advised, have an abundance of courage.

Their method of attacking formidable animals is their protection; for, instead of laying hold like the bulldog and terrier species, they only snap, and from the power of their enormous jaws, cut deep and severely at every essay. Over and over again I have laughed myself uncomfortable, to see the skill with which they would exhaust a wolf; their speed being very great, they would overhaul the prowler, and the first warning he would have of their vicinity would be a severe snap in the loins or hams. The wolf would then show fight, and as he would dash at one (which would nimbly avoid him), the other would make his tusks acquainted with the foe's flesh. On the approach of the hunter, Lupus would again make off, to be halted in the same peremptory and uncourteous manner, till the unfortunate wolf would be compelled to yield to circumstances and want of speed.

The only animal that these dogs are unsuccessful in overtaking is the antelope. The large hare of the plains (*Lepus Townsendii*), familiarly known as jackass rabbit (if unable to gain cover), will seldom go over three hundred yards before being picked up.

Although I never had a chance to try these hounds on a grizzly, there is no doubt but they could divert that formidable gentleman's attention, so as to afford the sportsman unusual opportunities for administering the *coup de grâce.*

For hard and fast riding I would recommend the common English hunting-saddle, although for travelling long distances, and carrying game or weighty additions, the American saddle is preferable. It would be well, therefore, to be provided with both; and as it can always be carried on the back of an unused animal, it will be seldom found in the way.

The exact locality to be certain to find buffalo is a difficult matter to say, as they are so erratic in their habits that a place where they have abounded one season will be found almost deserted next—the progress of vegetation, the severity of the weather, and the vicinity of war or hunting parties of Indians, having doubtless much influence; still, if I were about to revisit these sporting Elysiums, I would take myself to St. Louis, and go on board one of the numerous steamboats that start each spring on trading excursions for the Upper Missouri. There are few parts of the upper river where a landing cannot easily be effected, and your horses, by this means, can be placed fresh and in good condition where their labours are about to commence; independent of which a supply of grain can be taken along that will be invaluable in keeping your nags in good heart.

The vicinity of many of the forts is much to be recommended, for you will there have opportunities of making the acquaintance of numbers of the officers of the United States regular army, whose society, like that of all educated gentlemen, will do much to dissipate ennui and the monotony of camp-life in bad weather; moreover, there are many first-class hunters among them, and they are proverbial, as a body, for their hospitality and good social qualities, while from the numerous *attachés* that surround the forts, the most authentic and reliable information can always be obtained of the movements and *locale* of game.

CHAPTER XVIII.

THE MUSK SHEEP OF ARCTIC AMERICA.

WHY this animal should be designated ox is to me a mystery. Plainly do its appearance, habits, &c., designate it as a member of the *Ovis* family, instead of the *Bos*. However, Blainville, a naturalist of good reputation, to avoid censure, boldly seizes both, and designates it *Ovibos*, thereby claiming a distinct standing and title to the honour of its representing a new genus by adopting the *sobriquet* of two old ones. Audubon does likewise, and heads his chapters on these animals with the title of "Genus *Ovibos*." As an authority on American natural history, the latter is entitled to the highest consideration. At the same time I cannot help feeling that the name adopted is a shuffling pretext to prevent controversy, and the possibility of making a mistake that in future years would require to be corrected.

I have just returned from a most delightful party, the lion of which was a gentleman who for upwards of ten years had shut himself out of the civilised world, by residing upon one of the numerous lakes of North America, that are situated on the extreme edge of the Rocky Mountains and the barren lands in sixty-four or sixty-five degrees north latitude. Here the musk sheep (for I must call it so) is found occasionally, but when he progressed farther to the north-west it was no uncommon occurrence in a day's march to see several herds; in fact, they were so numerous that the camp was always well supplied with them for food. Their flesh he pronounces excellent and nutritious when fat, but quite the reverse when, by a long protracted winter, they become thin and attenuated. The flavour is much the same as that of venison, although much coarser in the grain, and is entirely free from any musky odour, except in very old males, and during the rutting season. The ground which they principally frequent is the same on which is found the small cariboo—immense stretches of rolling, rocky steppes, most sparsely supplied with vegetation, except where an occasional brook winds its solitary course towards some giant river, rapidly hurrying on its northern course to the Arctic Ocean. Their principal food is the various mosses, the leaves of stunted brush, and the fine velvety grasses that sparsely crop up in wet localities.

For animals so unwieldy in shape and appearance they are wonderfully nimble, making always for the roughest grounds when pursued, leaping with agility from rock to rock, and scaling the faces of slopes so perpendicular that the hunter, with hands and feet brought into play, finds it almost impossible to follow. Their hearing and sight are very acute; at the same time so suspicious and cautious are they that, although always assembled in little parties of from ten to twenty, sentinels are regularly told off for duty, which place themselves in the most commanding positions, ready to whistle the signal of alarm on the slightest suspicion of danger, accompanied by the usual sheep-like stamp of displeasure, which summons the herd to assist in inspecting the supposed intruder before they shift their feeding grounds for haunts that previous experience has taught them are more secure.

From the high latitudes in which they are found, Captain Parry, the celebrated voyager, classes them among the dwellers north of the Arctic circle; and well might he or others do so, for so well are they protected by nature from the inclement weather of the inhospitable regions which they inhabit, that the most severe snow and frost little interfere with the routine of their life. Their wool is remarkably soft, long, and densely close; so that at a small distance, if they are walking over irregular-surfaced soil, their feet are scarcely seen, the body of surrounding fringe giving the observer the impression which would arise if you saw an animal surrounded with a petticoat. Their colour is much the same as that of the buffaloes of the plains, possibly a little darker, and at a distance they might easily be mistaken for them; but on closer inspection the delusion cannot continue, for their outline of form, sheep-like movement and figure, at once corrects the error. In height they stand from eleven and a half to twelve and a half hands, the males being the largest and most cumbersome in appearance. Their legs are excessively short, and gifted with great muscular power, while the track of their hoof is about the size of a two-year-old steer's, but straighter and less pointed. The head is ornamented with handsome horns which almost unite at the base, and taper off with graceful, handsome sweeps to sharp points, which are generally in the mature animal on a level with the eyes. The nose is covered with soft downy hair, and the eye, which is large and full, gives the physiognomy an intelligent look, which would induce the belief that no great difficulty would occur to prevent their domestication. If such could be effected, great benefit might result from the introduction of their wool into our markets, as from its extreme length, elasticity, and fineness, it could be manufactured into the most superior class of cloths.

Their rutting season occurs at the breaking up of the autumn, when the cold and fitful winds of October commence to warn us that warmth is gone, and snow and ice are coming. The male, who generally is very inoffensive, unless he chance to receive a wound incapacitating him from escape, becomes now most quarrelsome and vindictive, attacking with the greatest fury whatever provokes his displeasure; and woe be to the white man or Indian who then meets him, if away from a place of escape or unprovided with fire-arms. At this time furious engagements take place among the males, which sometimes continue till one or both of the contestants are so much exhausted that they fall an easy prey to the Indian's arrows or the tusks of the northern large grey wolf.

In May the female produces a single lamb, over whose welfare the mother shows great solicitude. The young, until three or four weeks' old, are unable to follow the parent, but are hid away in the manner usual with deer; the old lady, however, on such occasions never wanders far from her offspring's hiding-place, and on the least suspicion of danger rushes to of their life. Their wool is remarkably soft, long, and densely close; so that at a small distance, if they are walking over irregular-surfaced soil, their feet are scarcely seen, the body of surrounding fringe giving the observer the impression which would arise if you saw an animal surrounded with a petticoat. Their colour is much the same as that of the buffaloes of the plains, possibly a little darker, and at a distance they might easily be mistaken for them; but on closer inspection the delusion cannot continue, for their outline of form, sheep-like movement and figure, at once corrects the error. In height they stand from eleven and a half to twelve and a half hands, the males being the largest and most cumbersome in appearance. Their legs are excessively short, and gifted with great muscular power, while the track of their hoof is about the size of a two-year-old steer's, but straighter and less pointed. The head is ornamented with handsome horns which almost unite at the base, and taper off with graceful, handsome sweeps to sharp points, which are generally in the mature animal on a level with the eyes. The nose is covered with soft downy hair, and the eye, which is large and full, gives the physiognomy an intelligent look, which would induce the belief that no great difficulty would occur to prevent their domestication. If such could be effected, great benefit might result from the introduction of their wool into our markets, as from its extreme length, elasticity, and fineness, it could be manufactured into the most superior class of cloths.

Their rutting season occurs at the breaking up of the autumn, when the cold and fitful winds of October commence to warn us that warmth is gone, and snow and ice are coming. The male, who generally is very inoffensive, unless he chance to receive a wound incapacitating him from escape, becomes now most quarrelsome and vindictive, attacking with the greatest fury whatever provokes his displeasure; and woe be to the white man or Indian who then meets him, if away from a place of escape or unprovided with fire-arms. At this time furious engagements take place among the males, which sometimes continue till one or both of the contestants are so much exhausted that they fall an easy prey to the Indian's arrows or the tusks of the northern large grey wolf.

In May the female produces a single lamb, over whose welfare the mother shows great solicitude. The young, until three or four weeks' old, are unable to follow the parent, but are hid away in the manner usual with deer; the old lady, however, on such occasions never wanders far from her offspring's hiding-place, and on the least suspicion of danger rushes to her lamb, prepared to do battle with all intruders, whatever may be their size or appearance. The droppings of these animals, with the exception of their size, exactly resemble those of sheep.

I will here relate two anecdotes told by Mr. McNabb, illustrative of the chances of accident that will occasionally occur to the sportsman, even when in pursuit of animals which are generally deemed harmless; and clearly proving how necessary presence of mind and decision of character are to the person who adopts wild life, or hopes to return safely from a trip to the comparatively unknown tracks of the great north-western portion of the American continent.

"The ice had just disappeared from the rivers; the wild duck had already arrived in immense numbers, so that our table daily had been graced with the choicest varieties, when a thought struck me that an alteration of fish for fowl would be most acceptable to the palates of the encampment. About a couple of miles distant, where the river, contracted to one-fourth its usual breadth, rushed into a noble pool, I had on the previous year been most successful; moreover, it was a pleasant pool to fish—no overhanging bushes, but gently sloping, gravelly banks nearly the entire length of its margin. In an hour I had secured more trout than I felt disposed to carry; so, work being over,

I treated myself to a pipe. While enjoying my baccy, a wader of a description I never before saw lit close to me. It was so tame that I threw several stones at it, almost with success, for the distance was not over ten or fifteen yards, before it took to wing, and went farther down the stream. Anxious to procure a new specimen, I followed till almost a mile lay between me and my fish. To save distance in returning, I determined to cut across the angle formed by the bend of the river, and had progressed about half the way when I saw a female musk-sheep coming after me. When a lad in the Highlands I had got dreadfully punished by a tup, and the remembrances of the event had not yet been forgotten. A mountain ram is a small beast compared to my present pursuer, and *he* was able to do enough mischief. The ground was very roughly sprinkled with boulders, some of great size, and for the most inaccessible of those I made the best speed I could muster, and only succeeded in gaining a place of safety when the ewe's horns were within a foot or two of my hurdies. For over an hour she kept watch on me; and, worse than all, when I got back to my fish some vermin or other had carried all the best ones off, and it was getting too late to hunt up its nest. When at home the Indians soon explained the reasons of this unprovoked attack, and proved the correctness of their assertion by shooting the mother next morning and bringing the lamb home, which we were unable to keep alive for over three days, much to the regret of all."

The second adventure is a repetition of the inexcusable folly of not immediately loading your gun before approaching wounded game. "In stalking some barren cariboo, eight musk sheep crossed directly between me and the deer. I was well hid at the time, so that they came unsuspiciously within thirty yards. In a moment I gave them both barrels. To the first shot an old buck dropped, and rolled into a ravine; the second barrel crippled a three-quarter grown sheep so badly that I knew less than a mile would lay her up. In my hurry to secure the old one, without loading I hurried to the ravine. There he was, as I thought, in the last struggle. Down I jumped into the hollow, which was about ten feet deep; but no sooner did he see me than up he got, and, head down, charged. I turned tail, and fortunately scrambled out a wiser man; for, deil tak' me, if ever I gang near any o' them without powther and lead baith in my gun."

The average weight of the full-grown male is about four hundred and fifty pounds, while the female is generally from fifty to seventy-five pounds less. The Indians state that they live to an immense age, which belief is probably caused by their venerable and ragged appearance at the time they cast their coats.

So little is known of this animal, and there are so very few who have had any experience of its habits, that I trust the readers of "Accessible Field Sports" will excuse my writing from the experience of others instead of from my own.

CHAPTER XIX.

SNIPE SHOOTING ON ILLINOIS PRAIRIES.

Who that is a sportsman, if he has time and means, can remain immersed in town or mercantile pursuits in this most prolific season of the year for field sports —spring? Consider only the contrast of winding your course along the solitary brook, bubbling and leaping with impetuous energy over its rocky course, and singing lullabies of soft music so soothing to the mind, while Nature, as if revived from her winter's rest, sends forth odours so suggestive of returning summer; or, on the other hand, wandering over the boundless prairie, drinking into your very soul the invigorating breeze surcharged with vitality and health, instead of being seated with the constant pens, ink, and paper before you, the incessant hum caused by toiling life grating on your ears, and the everlasting mental excitement of the busy world resting upon you.

SNIPE SHOOTING.

Last season but one, on the prairies, I shot snipe day after day, till a surfeit might have been expected, and only desisted when the advancement of the season proclaimed the approach of the period for breeding; and, though some might imagine such a lengthened campaign would have sufficed for coming years, before twelve months had slipped past I stretched my arms, looked at the sky, observed the wind, all three of which being favourable, anathematised, perhaps, the destiny or fate that compelled me to accept more sedentary town occupation.

With that intuitive feeling that tells the swallow when to migrate, the fish a change of weather, or the cattle the portended storm—we feel certain that all the southern prairies of Illinois are now alive (March) with snipe, that they are lying well to the gun, and that heavy bags are being made. We can even shut our eyes and imagine that we are just approaching some favourite spot either bordering on a slough or stream, or rich-loamed dip between swelling slopes, and that the game is flushing right and left, as we cautiously pursue our course down wind, while our trusty and well-tried gun rapidly responds to our aim. Again and again we fill and empty our blood-stained pockets, till the body, from fatigue, calls "Hold, enough!" or we return, with waning day, to our little bald-faced pony, ever ready with a neigh to welcome his master's re-appearance. Though to revisit these secluded haunts, to re-enact these scenes, may not be my lot, why should they not be the reader's? If you have courage to discharge a gun, you will find abundance to shoot at. If you are a proficient in the art, you will make such a bag of snipe as an English sportsman scarcely ever dreamt of, embellished with numerous duck, teal, and, possibly, curlew; and if you are a true disciple of the virgin goddess, you will enjoy more real pleasure than probably ever was your fortune. Go, by all means —do not stop to hesitate—and I will guarantee you an amount of sport that will induce many a future return.

Those gentlemen who live in the cities that surround these sporting localities, are well aware of the excellence of the shooting at this season upon the prairies, and make up large parties to have a week or so at the Wilson snipe, erroneously called Jack snipe. In the course of a day's shooting I have met visitors from Louisville, Cincinnati, and St. Louis, marching like companies in skirmishing order, and keeping up a regular fusillade. But so great is the extent of hunting-ground, and so numerous the game, that in each day, over the same beat, no visible diminution can be observed. We do not mean to say that no English sportsman ever made a trial of these western haunts, but we are thoroughly impressed that the excellence of these grounds is far from as widely known as it deserves, and that many persons possessed both with means and inclination are unaware that within thirty-six hours' journey of New York they can have such snipe shooting as is to be enjoyed in no other portion of the globe.

As to all the haunts of snipe, the visitors must go well prepared with a good supply of water-proof boots, for the walking is always damp, sometimes wet; also a good stock of flannel clothing will be found indispensable, for at this season the weather is frequently so variable, that although noon may be oppressively warm, sunset and the hour of the tramp home—especially if your feet are wet may be found sufficiently cold to chill the warmest blood. As the ground frequently is very destitute of cover, the birds will not lie for a dog to set them; nor does this matter, the snipe being so abundant; but a good retriever, who will keep well to heel, and is under perfect control, will be useful. Moreover, few days will pass without several duck which you have killed or disabled falling in the adjoining sloughs, which, without a retriever or a wading escapade, would inevitably be lost.

In our opinion, there is no kind of field sport in which the breech-loader so plainly shows its superiority over the old muzzle-gun as in snipe shooting. From our experience of the past season, unless compelled, we should never use any other for this description of sport. The rapidity with which they can both be loaded and cleaned, dispensing with the ramrod, which is always difficult to handle in cold weather, being able to load without placing the butt on the ground or in the mud, and the non-necessity of using caps, are advantages in all sporting, but in none more decided than in snipe shooting.

At first when the snipe arrive, they are poorer in flesh, and wilder than further on in the season; but if the day should be mild and the sun warm, they will almost lie to be tramped upon, and when flushed only fly a few yards before lighting. In fact, you will frequently have trouble to get them to take wing if the cover chance to be good. But for choice, the snipe generally prefer the bare ground which has been burned over during the fall or winter, or has been overflowed by the rising of some neighbouring river, the alluvial surface deposit apparently suiting them better to bore in.

As an estimate of what may be considered a good day's sport at this season of the year on these grounds, we will recur to our own experience, and only state facts. An acquaintance, who was a good shot, killed, to our certain knowledge, nine dozen snipe in seven hours, and we ourselves have frequently killed from seven to eight dozen in the same time. The first day's shooting of my last season, over indifferent ground, and very difficult to walk upon from its inequality of surface, in five hours I to my own gun bagged four dozen, and but that the birds were extremely wild, would possibly have knocked over fifty per cent. more.

Where we should advise the shooter commencing snipe shooting in spring would be at Vincennes, on the Ohio and Mississippi railroad. From here you can have sport in every direction, and when you feel desirous of change of scene, the prairies, which begin here and continue north almost uninterruptedly to the great lakes, will be found abundantly stocked from the date of the arrival of the first flight of the migratory hordes. Of one thing we should like to caution the novice; viz., the using of too large shot. No. 9 will be found the best. A snipe requires but little hitting to bring him down, and then his body is so small, that at the distance of forty yards, although your aim may be correct, if you shoot large shot, it is far from improbable that the game may fly through it. Of course, it would be well, particularly when using a breech-loader, to carry a few cartridges of No. 5, in case you come across duck, for the facility with which you can withdraw one charge and substitute another, is one of the great points of excellence which the new gun possesses over the old pattern. Moreover, when your day's work is over and your domicile reached, if you are careful of your ammunition and dislike throwing away a couple of charges, you can extract your cartridges in a moment. Persons residing in the country often deem it necessary to retain at least one gun in the house loaded, for the reason, that if you should be suddenly called upon to shoot some marauding hawk which is decimating the hen-roost, the delay of loading would be fatal to any chance of killing the bloodthirsty scoundrel. Still, at all times, particularly if there are children about, loaded guns are most objectionable; but if you chance to be possessed of a breech-loader, this is obviated, for the gun can be loaded almost instantaneously. It is of such frequent occurrence to read in our public papers accounts of frightful accidents, resulting from strangers or youths playing with loaded arms, that we should feel thankful that at length such an invention has been perfected, as will at least reduce, if not totally abolish, these heart-rending misfortunes.

If your frame be cast in that iron mould which nature has bestowed on some, and you are consequently capable of bearing, without inconvenience, fatigue and exposure, and are, at the same time, desirous of making as heavy a bag as possible, while shooting over your snipe beat, pay particular attention to the watercourses and sloughs, and when you become satisfied that you have found a spot where the ducks are in the habit of spending their evenings, which may be ascertained by the down-trodden weeds and muddy appearance of the water, mark the place, for when it becomes too late to continue peppering the snipe, you can return and lie in ambush for the web-footed gentry. Duck, from flying high when on the move, can be seen much later than small game (which, being flushed on the ground, head away from you, parallel to it), more particularly if watching for them, as you can frequently get them against some clear spot in the sky. Frequently, I have killed in half an hour half-a-dozen of that prince of birds and epicurean dainties, the mallard, in this manner, when it was so dark that, after they had dropped, but for the sagacity of my retriever I was scarcely aware whether I had correctly aimed. If the evening should be dark and loomy, with indications of change to cold weather, and a high wind blowing, it will be unnecessary to wait as late as sunset before visiting the feeding ground of the duck; for, under such circumstances, we have known them to come in fearlessly early in the afternoon. However, you cannot practise this work successfully without some kind of screen, which will require to be larger and thicker if your clothes do not in colour closely approximate the hue of the ground.

Brother sportsmen, let me once more advise you to take this western trip, and on your return I know I shall receive your thanks for being the means of introducing you to sport that cannot fail to rejoice the heart of every true lover of the dog and gun.

CHAPTER XX.

HINTS FOR AMERICAN SHOOTING.

No breed of dog combines so thoroughly as the setter the following three important points: speed, endurance, and beauty of form. The greyhound may be more swift, but he lacks the endurance; the foxhound may be as lasting, but he falls far short in personal appearance and sagacity.

Some sportsmen prefer the pointer; for general purposes, give me the setter; for hard work and constant shooting, in America I would have no other. If you are the happy possessor of a pure, good breed, you will seldom or never know the annoyance of sore feet, and the frequent consequent loss of a good day's sport, as their paws are well protected against the sharp wire grasses of the prairies by the quantity of hair growing between their toes, and around their pads. In briers, thorns, and thick covers generally, he again shows his superiority, owing to his being defended by the thickness of his coat, enabling him to penetrate thickets that a pointer will scarcely look at. For a person who shoots but seldom, and that over a smooth country, the pointer is good, on account of his less high-strung disposition; but for the hard-working, indefatigable sportsman, who finds a variety of game upon his beat, where a retriever, both by land and water, is sometimes necessary, the smooth-coated dog cannot be compared to his feathered brother. With regard to which of the two has the best nose, the balance of opinion will be found in favour of the pointer; but this idea has, in a majority of cases, been hastily adopted. It has, no doubt, arisen from the greater inclination which the pointer manifests to point, and from over docility dwelling on places which birds have left some time, and which a setter will scarcely notice. This circumstance, however, causes me to think quite the reverse, the superior scenting powers of the latter informing him that the game has gone. The better, and, perhaps, the best method of determining this point is, to observe which has the superiority on bad-scenting days, or in retrieving a wounded bird; but in England setters and pointers are not broken to retrieve; in America no dog is considered perfect without these qualifications.

I am aware that many are as ardent supporters of

the pointer as I am of the setter, but I speak not from hastily-formed opinions, but long experience, having owned both; in fact, once I thought the opposite to what I do now, but at that period I did not as constantly shoot, being only occasionally able to get a few days in the field at a time, and then the adage of "once broken, always broken," so frequently applied to the pointer, was verified, while the setters, from want of work and exuberance of spirit, would, during the first half-hour, perhaps, behave badly, and require rating both with voice and whip, causing annoyance and the probable loss of one or two shots. But then look at the performance of both on the second or third day. Master Don, the pointer, walks at heel sore-footed and crest-fallen, while Beau, the setter, ranges indefatigably both far and near, neither deterred on his beat by rough·ground, briers, nor marsh.

All the prairies of the Western States are well stocked with pinnated grouse, familiarly called Prairie Chicken, but they abound principally in Central and Northern Illinois, Iowa, and Northern Missouri. They feed on berries and the tender tops and seeds of grasses. They pair early in the spring, and the female lays from eight to fifteen eggs, in a very primitive nest on the ground. The young leave the nest almost as soon as hatched, and continue to follow the hen, till the frosty nights in autumn set in, when they unite in packs of frequently as many as a hundred brace. They continue thus packed in the greatest harmony till the approach of spring, when amorous feelings assert the mastery over social amity, and fierce battles ensue between the males, seldom resulting in the wounding and maiming of either of the combatants. On one occasion, while riding over some burnt land on one of the southern prairies of Illinois, on my way to a slough to kill some ducks in the evening flight, I observed two chickens engaged in fierce combat; they permitted me to approach and capture both, thoroughly exhausted, but unmarked by any wound. The care and assiduity of the female for the protection of her young are truly wonderful; if she sees danger approach her brood, she will throw herself on the ground, screaming and manifesting an apparent incapacity of escape; but when she has drawn the enemy a sufficient distance from her chicks, she leaves the astonished intruder to follow her only with his eyes.

Chicken shooting is laborious, requiring both judgment and experience to be eminently successful, particularly when you happen to be a stranger in the locality; and the season being generally the hottest in the year, September, it is absolutely necessary to be clothed in the lightest attire. A flannel shirt and drawers are undoubtedly indispensable, as this material is a bad conductor of heat, and if habituated to it you will experience no increase of warmth; at the same time it will most effectually absorb the perspiration, and prevent your catching cold. Long boots up to the knee should also be used, as they will effectually guard you against snakes, of which there are no scarcity among the long, rank grass, through which you have frequently to walk. To those who may be troubled with tender feet I would advise a little tallow rubbed on the joints before starting in the morning, and a foot-bath of strong salt and water on their return. This method I have never known to fail when strictly attended to. On no account should the sportsman drink the water lying in the low grounds, as fever and ague are in every draught; but cold tea, or a weak dilution of whiskey and water, will be found a good and serviceable beverage. The former I particularly recommend.

Immediately after feeding in the morning, and about the time the dew leaves the grass, the birds go to the low and damp grounds, soon afterwards is the proper time to commence the day's sport. From that time, on the edge of the streams or wet ground, till the extreme heat of the day comes, good shooting may be obtained, and also from three o'clock, when the birds again revisit the low grounds, to an hour before sunset, at which time you should make the utmost speed to the wheat stubbles, where you can generally shoot till so dark that you have difficulty in distinguishing your game. If you are disinclined to lose the meridian hours, and feel strong enough to stand the oppressive influence of a noonday sun, the rolling high grounds, or barren, loose-soiled places, where moulding and scratching *à la* tame fowl can be enjoyed, will be found the *locale;* but I would advise all, if they have no regard for themselves, to have some consideration for their canine favourites, for, remember, for one mile you tramp they go ten, and if they feel exhausted with their morning's work, they are incapable of expressing their fatigue.

In hunting any description of game in which you make use of the dog as an assistant to find it, be careful to give him the wind, and never hurry or force him forward when he shows an indication of winding birds; remember he knows infinitely better than you do, and that he has some cogent reason to act as he does; and further, that he has not learned the diplomatic art of lying, although his accomplishments may be numerous and varied. The sportsman who beats his ground slowly and carefully will invariably kill more than he who is always hurrying on as if he were the wearer of the time-honoured seven-leagued boots. On one occasion, when in company with a city friend, our dogs kept drawing, and occasionally pointing across a stubble, both of us following close behind; when we reached the opposite fence, he proposed, in a manner that would not brook contradiction, to go to some birds we had previously marked down. He went, while I continued to beat the lower angle of the field, which had so far been neglected; the result was that I killed eleven, while Mr. Obstinate only got a wild shot as a recompense for his haste and want of perseverance.

On finding a pack, the old birds are generally the first to take wing. Kill them if you can, and the remainder will be easily accounted for. Without the knowledge and trickery of mature years, they will remain when marked down almost to be kicked from beneath your dog's nose, and, in nine cases out of ten, flush singly.

No country takes more out of dogs than the prairie; therefore I should strongly recommend that two brace be provided, the one couple to be hunted in the forenoon, the other in the after part of the day; by changing them thus, they will be sufficiently strong and fresh to do good work as long as you can walk to them.

Burning the prairies, when performed in the spring

is very injurious and destructive, for by this means numbers of nests are annually destroyed; yet the practice will be continued, on account of the benefit derived by the owners of the soil, as the ashes manure the ground, and cause the pasture to come in early and luxuriant. As a general rule, you will always in the commencement of the season find the prairie fowl in the vicinity of stubble fields, where they invariably feed night and morning. Frequently they perch upon fences or stacks of grain, and will often suffer the sportsman to approach within easy gun-shot; but he that would avail himself of this ignoble means of swelling his bag, should be avoided by his fellow mortals, and condemned to wander the remainder of his days in a *terra incognita* swarming with mosquitoes and black flies, bed bugs and snakes. Late in the season, when the birds have packed and cease to lie well to the dog, the only time that you can hope to be successful is when the sun has reached his greatest altitude and strength; then, on the grassy slopes directly facing his genial rays, they often appear, for an hour or two, to become indolent or reckless of their safety, remaining so close that they will flush within easy gun-shot, or early in the morning, or late in the evening, when, if you hide yourself in a fence corner, you will get frequent shots at them as they wing their way to corn-fields to feed.

I remember in the month of November, in Newton County, Indiana, killing over a dozen in this manner, in less than an hour, when waiting for wild duck. Pot hunters and game dealers' emissaries have numerous and successful ways of destroying this noble bird all the year round; but with their shameful practices I have nothing to do, hoping that all who pretend to or appropriate the name of sportsmen in America, will show their disapproval of such outrages by hunting from a neighbourhood, wherever they have influence, these ignoble slaughterers, who will, more than aught else, tend to ultimately banish from the accessible grounds one of the handsomest and largest of the grouse family.

CHAPTER XXI.

SHOOTING IN MISSOURI.

ACCORDING to advice, my friends and self tried Brookfield, on the Hannibal and St. Joseph's railroad, in the State of Missouri, three years ago, and found the locality as represented. The hotel at the railroad station is well kept, and if the culinary department does not suit its visitors they must be very fastidious. Moreover, there is not a house of public entertainment that I know of, in America, where there is a more evident desire on the part of employer and domestics to do all in their power for the accommodation of their guests, and to render them comfortable. Game, I am assured by those who reside there, is unusually abundant this year (1869), and they attribute as a reason that, during the war, guerillas were so numerous that few had the hardihood of risking the loss of their guns, or, possibly, being roughly handled, whatever their love of field sports might have been, so that little shooting was then done. But, fortunately, those days are over, and the peaceful sportsman can wander about at large without the slightest fear of molestation. Besides the usual game birds, on my trip I killed several deer, and if I had previously known that they were so numerous would have paid them an earlier visit. A circumstance occurred to me the third day after arrival, which, I think, all will say is unusual; at least, in my long experience, I cannot remember having seen the same, viz., wild turkeys lying to a dog. A large hawk was hovering in the neighbourhood at the time, and to his unwelcome presence I attribute this piece of fortune. With hounds admirable sport could here be obtained, for the greater portion of the ground is rideable, and the land covered with brush, neither too thick nor tall to impede the progress of a good horse. However, let me call attention to an abuse which exists here, as well as in many more of the Western States —the capturing of partridges with the net. American gentlemen ought to do something to stop this barbarous practice,—one which, in a few years, if continued, will ultimately ruin their finest shooting grounds. To attempt to curtail what the people here deem their privilege is no easy matter; however, such people as are guilty of this heinous offence are, in nine instances out of ten, worthless village loafers, too lazy to work, and earning a precarious existence by supplying city markets with their victims. Shooting, I insist, invigorates the frame, strengthens the mind, and is, without doubt, a most harmless pleasure, encouraging persons to goodfellowship and unselfish intercourse, inducing all the good traits of character to be enlarged, and the baser to be depressed; therefore the facilities for legitimate shooting should be encouraged, and game protected, by such wholesome laws as will enable future generations to enjoy this superlative pleasure.

CHAPTER XXII.

A LONG DEER HUNT.

To kill deer, if you come across them, is easy enough, or to knock them over if they are driven past your stand is what any schoolboy can do, provided he keeps cool; but to stalk deer with success, alone and unaided, requires as much practice, twice the experience, and four times the cuteness and observation requisite for any other description of field sport.

I once knew a man who was pretty nearly master of this art, and he could as well discriminate a good day for deer stalking from an indifferent one as he could a thoroughbred from a mustang. "No use going out to-day, Cap.," he would say, in answer to an inquiry; "the woodpeckers have got their heads up, and the deer are lying: best stop at home;" and best it always was. Now, after acknowledging myself not to be an expert, I hope the reader will deal gently with me, as I am desirous of relating a little episode that took place when my experience was far from being as great as it is now.

As deer in the Eastern States of America are nearly exterminated, my friends will have, at least in imagination, to believe themselves transported to the grand and luxuriant West, to no less a locality than the Wabash Valley, in Southern Illinois, where the soil is rich and fat, the timber heavy, and corn sometimes reaches fifteen feet in height; where the atmosphere is redolent of miasma and fever; where the inhabitants shake half the time with chills, and their complexions resemble yellow ochre, with a little of its brilliancy extracted; where, half the year, floods cut you off from the rest of the world, and you are compelled to become a boatman or a Robinson Crusoe, whether you like it or not. However, good fellows, with big, kind hearts, are to be found here; and if anything in this world can compensate, which I doubt, for loss of health, I am inclined to believe that it is the *bon camerade* of a genial spirit. But times are changed since the date I name; the skilful, good, kind, little doctor of the district—a host in himself—has departed for the land of gold; the hunter, my companion—a Dutchman by name but not by nature—retired, possibly, to his favourite Yazoo bottom, in Arkansas, to re-awaken its extensive woods with the echo of his deadly rifle, and cheer the many-spotted pack to their prey with his musical stentorian voice. By-the-bye, one remains—a German gentleman, whose convivial habits and goodness of heart, with courteous behaviour, will always endear him to those persons who can appreciate such praiseworthy traits. The better to enter into the spirit of the thing, I will transfer you to the neighbourhood —Vincennes, Indiana,—so that you may learn the characteristic features, and if, the first time you are travelling westward by the Ohio and Mississippi line of rail, you look out of the carriage window, after rumbling over the long Wabash bridge, and take a good view of the surroundings, know that this is the locality over which Ubique once hunted.

It was in the month of December or January, I cannot precisely state which, but on rising from my bed, to my surprise I found the ground covered with a few inches of snow, just sufficient, and none to spare, to track a deer with a degree of certainty. Now, I was hungry for venison, and such a chance was not to be let slip. From a habit which is unaccountable among many when they go from home, I had a morning cocktail brewed, and with a glass in each hand sought the dormitory of my Yazoo friend, and over the drinks we both discussed the prospects and our plan of campaign.

The horses were ordered to be in readiness after breakfast; buck-shot and bullets were hunted out, shooting boots greased, and 'baccy and pocket pistols loaded to the neck and stuffed in our saddle bags. A hard day we knew to be before us, so ample justice was done to our meal; for, gentlemen sportsmen, rely upon what I say, nothing so materially assists to withstand fatigue and cold as an ample breakfast.

A ride of about five miles took us to our ground, but our horses were fresh, and we impatient to be at work, consequently the distance was soon traversed, and we dismounted in a grove of saplings, well suited to hitch to and shelter the nags from the wintry blast.

While we are performing the necessary operation of loading, a description of our armament will not be inappropriate. Will, or so I'll call him, had an old, uncouth rifle, which, although possessed of no finish, could shoot "plumb centre," with the old-fashioned, double trigger, the second to set the hair-spring,—an invention I had seldom previously seen and never used; while I myself had my trusty double-barrel ten-bore, which, from long experience and association, I was aware had only to be held straight to do correct work.

A large swamp, about half a mile off, was a favourite

resort for deer, and to it we directed our steps; but before we had gone half the distance, we came across numerous tracks, so fresh that we kept a sharp lookout in all directions, hoping every moment to be gratified with the sight of some antlered monarch. Failing in this, we changed our tactics, friend Will posting me on the margin of a branch of the swamp, with my back against the butt of a tree, with instructions to remain still and keep a sharp look-out, while he would take a tour around, and possibly drive some stragglers across the run which my stand commanded. Slowly, after Will started, the time passed; the forest appeared perfectly deserted; not a squirrel or bird showed itself to break the monotony, except an angry, squabbling family of woodpeckers, who appeared to have some serious disagreement in reference to the possession of a hole in the trunk of a dead giant tree. Wet feet are never conducive to comfort, and much less so when you are prevented from taking exercise; besides, it was bitterly cold. First I stood on one leg, then on the other, after the manner of geese, which birds I began to consider I much resembled, till at last the inaction became so unendurable that I was very nearly taking up my gun and starting in pursuit of my supposed recreant friend.

As I was about to put my resolution in practice, I

thought I heard a voice, and on looking in the direction from whence it proceeded, I was surprised to see a couple of hunters with a cur dog passing my retreat, about a hundred yards off. He who has shot much in the timber, well knows that if he remains quiet the possibility is great that those moving about may make the game start towards his retreat. And well it was I did so; for ere five minutes had passed a grand old turkey, head down, and going like a race-horse, shot by; but turkey was not deer, so I let him go, preferring to be without turkey to braving the wrath of Will for firing at illegitimate game. How often patience and forbearance receive their reward! and so it was in this instance, for scarcely had the gobbler gone by when a fine large buck hove in sight. From his manner he was evidently alarmed, for every now and then he would stop, snort, and continue his route. Unfortunately, he was heading so as to pass too far off to afford a good shot, and the ground was too clear to permit me, with any prospect of success, to better my position; so I had almost made up my mind not to shoot. However, I changed my resolution, for as soon as he came abreast of me, he halted, and looked around. The temptation I could no longer withstand; so, pitching my gun with due elevation, I let drive the first barrel, but with no apparent result, for the deer only threw up his head and trotted off. The second barrel I quickly determined to put in, and holding well in front and high, had the satisfaction of seeing his lordship make a tremendous bound and drop his flag, a certain indication that some of the shot had taken effect, but the distance was so great that successful results could scarcely be expected.

Nothing is so difficult as to obtain a gun that throws buck-shot well. I am inclined to believe that gun-makers have not paid the same amount of attention to discovering the proper internal construction of barrels, so as to obtain the greatest range and closeness in throwing this description of projectile. Generally, at the distance of one hundred yards, the side of a barn would be none too large a target to be certain of hitting; and again, occasionally a barrel will make an unusually good pattern at one discharge, while at the next it will be quite the reverse, so that hitting a deer at a hundred yards I consider more the result of luck than good guiding, if charged with buck-shot.

After waiting for nearly a quarter of an hour I was joined by my friend, who at once inquired what I had shot at; but when I told him the distance, he only laughed one of those peculiar, little dry laughs which, as plainly as words, said, "You're a fool if you expect to eat any of that carcass." Nevertheless, we together inspected the track, and I had not even the gratification to find blood. Well, Will was for giving it up, but I wanted to follow it out; and after using all his powers of persuasion and argument in favour of his views, my friend succumbed, and consented for once to be dictated to.

For over a mile we followed our game. The line was straight and the tracks distinct; moreover, the gait was steady, if one could judge from the regularity of the impressions; and there was nought to indicate that we might not with as great propriety follow any animal in these bottom lands that had never had a shot fired at him. Will was going ahead, leading, and your humble servant bringing up the rear, when the former suddenly halted and turned round. From the expression of his face I knew something was up, but was scarcely prepared for the information he gave. "Look here," said Will; "you have hit that deer, Cap., tolerably badly, and I suspect we shall get him yet; his fore leg is disabled, and he can't travel far without our overhauling him." On inquiring how he gained his information, he pointed to the tracks; and sure enough the off fore-foot, instead of making a clean impression, cut the snow for nearly a foot both before and after. "You see," said he, chuckling, "he don't use both alike, for it's all he can do to get this one clear of the ground." There was no gainsaying such conclusive evidence, and with renewed ardour we sharpened up the pace of pursuit, alternately changing places, one being constantly on the look-out while the other tracked. Once or twice we got sight of the deer, but too far off, or for too limited a period, to shoot; but the view was always cheering. Forward we pressed, exultingly hoping that each minute would finish the hunt; but the deer thought otherwise, for he was of a most unaccommodating disposition. Soon it became apparent that the confounded brute was travelling the same circle, and that, unless we altered our plans, we might be kept going till dark; but as we were not disposed to work harder than necessary, it was agreed that I should drop behind and take up my stand beside the most eligible place, while Will continued the pursuit with the hope of driving our wily foe past my ambush. Though the plan was well devised, it failed in execution; for after an hour's tedious delay my companion rejoined me, disgusted and dispirited, heaping anathemas upon the foe, pronouncing him to be one of the very ugliest brutes he had ever come across. After all our trouble, it would never do thus to be defeated; so I proposed doing the tracking while he took a stand, at the same time changing guns at his request.

Full of hope, and animated with the desire of distinguishing myself, I pushed forward with renewed energy. At first the trail was tolerably clear, but, after some time, it led and twisted in every direction through innumerable hog paths. Never was I so sorely puzzled to keep correct, but with perseverance and care I managed to carry the track almost across to clear ground, where I suddenly lost all signs, and was completely brought to a stand-still. I was aware that all dodges were practised, more particularly when deer feel the effects of increasing weakness and incapacity for further exertion; so, hoping that fortune would favour me, I determined, like a skilful foxhunter, to make a cast completely round the disturbed ground. After the loss of twenty minutes I fortunately again struck the trail, which, to my surprise, led in a reverse direction; clearly indicating that the deer had retraced his steps probably in the same track, and thus, by this cunning device, almost succeeded in eluding his pursuers. The trail of the animal now became more irregular, and the tell-tale track of the wounded limb greatly assisted me in distinguishing his footsteps from those of his fellows, which on every opportunity he selected; but, all having failed to throw me off so far, the deer adopted a new ruse, which under other circumstances would have been eminently agreeable to the sportsman, but in this instance made me so savage that I would have indulged in the amiable weakness of breaking the gun-stock over the nearest tree, if it had not been that my friend might not see the joke of his gun being thus treated.

So intent was I in watching the tracks that I did not observe the exhausted deer had halted. Becoming alarmed by my near approach, and deeming it advisable to make a fresh effort to place distance between us, he again put forth renewed energy. The brush, unfortunately, was so remarkably dense, that although I got several glimpses of his tawny hide, still never for sufficient length of time to get a fair chance to shoot, and I was unwillingly compelled to keep tracking. About fifty yards from where I stood a small river, not over ninety feet across, named the Ambaras, wound its sluggish, peaceful way towards its parent stream, the Wabash, and direct for the nearest part of this river the deer had gone. Still I could not bring myself to believe that a buck at this season, with plenty of ice in the water, would hazard an aquatic performance; but my doubts were soon solved, for on reaching the margin, with surprise I saw the deer upon the ledge of ice attached to the bank struggling violently to keep his footing, the disabled leg, which appeared to hang powerless, evidently now causing serious inconvenience to his progress over the slippery surface. Such an opportunity to finish my work was not to be neglected, so cocking the rifle I pitched it forward and drew a bead, but still no report followed. All my power and exertion could not pull the trigger. Again and again I looked at the lock, and essayed another effort, but with the same result. At length, in despair, I desisted, and the deer, having altered his mind, came ashore and disappeared through the tangled brake. Of course, to examine the gun and inform myself what was wrong was my first thought. My surprise may be well imagined when, with all my endeavours, I could not get the hammer down; there it would stand, not a particle of compromise was in the confounded thing. All my skill in mechanism was called into play, all my past experience put to use, and not until my patience was nearly exhausted did I discover the use of the second trigger. Discouraged I was, but whether most at my own stupidity or want of luck I know not. Still hoping for another chance, I followed on in no very amiable frame of mind.

Time fled and the long shadows of the trees told of the rapid approach of night, still not a sight did I further get of the buck; and to add to my troubles, the tracks a second time led through ground that hogs had lately fed over. Never was I so sorely puzzled.

Back and forwards I searched, my eyes nearly strained to bursting, till at length I was compelled to give up the chase. On looking round to find out as nearly as possible my situation, the better and more directly to return to my horse, I espied a splendid wild turkey busy feeding not over thirty yards off, and still unaware of my presence. Sheltering myself behind a fallen log, I took sight along my barrel, determining inwardly to have some reward for my labour; but, although this time I worked the trigger correctly, nothing but the explosion of the cap took place; in fact, the rifle had missed fire. The turkey, frightened at the noise, lowered his head, ran about twenty yards, then stopped, and looked around, still ignorant of the cause of his alarm. Substituting a new cap and again taking sight, was but the work of a few moments, but still the gun refused to explode. I now sprung my ramrod and placed on the nipple another cap, but the result was as before, and the turkey having become conscious that he was in a dangerous neighbourhood, sought safety in flight. How often a day's shooting is one tissue of bad luck from morning till night! and so it was in this case. First, the game had passed too far from my stand; secondly, changing guns had lost me the deer; and thirdly, the carelessness of my friend in not sheltering his gun from the damp was the reason of my not having turkey for a future day's dinner.

Tired, hungry, and bad tempered, I struck off direct for my horse, expecting to have little more than a mile to walk; but with surprise, after having travelled that distance, I found I was turned round and lost. Already it was sunset, half an hour more would make it dark, and the bottom land which I was now wandering through, was as intricate, densely covered a swamp as ever was inhabited by wild cat. The season of the year, moreover, was not exactly the one to be selected for making your couch on the surface of mother earth, and visions of a good dinner, comfortable fire, and dry clothes floated before me. Hark! what is that—a dog barking? And so it was. Forward I pushed to the sound, and in doing so came across a road, which, on inspection, I recognised as one we had traversed in the morning. The rest of the programme for that day was plain sailing. I found my pony where he was left, my friend's horse being gone; so, concluding Will had made tracks for home, I mounted my fiery little nag, and with a sufficiently tight rein to guard against accidents, rattled home, almost at racing pace. It was nearly two hours afterwards that Will turned up wet and exhausted—down upon his luck and deer in particular—vowing that he would be up with the sun in the morning, and not return till he could boast of not having been beaten by a broken-legged deer, when there was enough snow to track. My defeat had similarly operated on myself, so that we mutually agreed to devote the morrow, blow or snow, to re-establish our tarnished honour. The morning was well suited for our task, still and clear, with just sufficient frost in the atmosphere to give zest to travelling. The track was easily found, my back track being taken as the guide to where I had my adventure with the turkey.

In ten minutes we again had our game afoot, but without getting a shot, the animal having doubled round before lying down, and, consequently, rising behind us. The bed where he had passed the night was soiled with blood, and other indications were such as to justify us in hoping early success. Although perseverance is generally rewarded, it was not so on this occasion. Hour after hour slipped by, the game appeared to moderate its pace in accordance with ours, just keeping sufficiently far ahead to be out of range. The badness of the walking (for a thaw had commenced), the continued disappointment, and the difficulty of following through the bush, commenced to operate upon our spirits, and, but that we struck a more open range of country where the travelling was better, doubtless we wou'd have given up. However, as we were in the vicinity of our ponies, we determined to continue the pursuit on horseback, hoping to get a view, in crossing some opening, where we could give the buck a run of a few minutes, with the expectation that a sharper gait might break him down; but luck continued adverse. Time was rapidly gliding by, a few hours more would bring on night, and, as far as we could see, the prospect of a termination was as distant as ever. Want of success or fatigue made us careless, and as we slowly wended our unthankful way—first one in front, then the other, unsportsmanlike on such occasions, talking aloud, deploring our misfortune, and paying but little attention to the surroundings—my pony (for I was in front) suddenly shied, turning almost completely round, and at the same time bringing me excessively near getting a spill. And what do you imagine was the cause of this want of propriety in so experienced a steed? Simply this: the deer had lain down, and we had almost ridden over him. To wheel round and try to bring my gun to bear was the work of a few seconds, but all my exertions and rapidity of motion were thrown away. The pony would not stand still; he had evidently been frightened, or perhaps was still in ignorance of what caused the alarm.

Moreover, my manœuvring so directly intervened between my friend and the deer that, for fear of peppering me, he dared not fire. To turn round and look at one another, first sulkily, but afterwards to burst into a roar of laughter at the absurdity of the whole thing, was the result, each agreeing that the buck had well earned his safety, and that two such awkward devils had no right to a feast of venison resulting from that hunt, and, therefore, we had better acknowledge that we were beaten handsomely, and that by a buck on three legs.

CHAPTER XXIII.

THE SPLIT BAMBOO FLY-RODS.

READER, have you ever had the misfortune to be caught in a provincial town, where you have no acquaintances, by such a wet day as confines you, *nolens volens*, to the limited accommodation of your hotel? Such has been my luck twice, and the minutes, seconds, and hours on each occasion appeared at least double the length of those of ordinary times. Such a miserable ordeal was almost forced upon me a month or two since; in fact, I had almost made up my mind to spend the intervening time between lunch and dinner with a book and pipe, when the constant interruptions I suffered from the impudent, obtrusive servants drove me to a state of desperation, so, seizing my hat and umbrella, I sallied forth, scarcely knowing where to direct my steps to obtain a few hours' peace and amusement. Suddenly, I was struck with the idea,—Why not go down to Messrs. Clerk and Co., Maiden Lane, and see what progress they are making with the split bamboo fly-rods my piscatorial friends in England are looking so anxiously forward for. Acting on the impulse of the moment, I jumped into a street car, and soon reached my destination. A fishing-tackle establishment has always been to me a place of great attraction. True, I had been at this one several times before, but never with sufficient spare time to overhaul and examine the numerous objects of interest that there, on every hand, surround you, with that attention and care that each deserved. And as the proprietors had always been civil and kind on previous visits, I doubted not that they would pardon my prying curiosity. Reaching the front of the establishment, which has its *spécialité* well marked by an immense rod projecting over the pavement, a show-case filled with flies of every size and colour, artificial baits so numerous that they must be nameless, reels, flies, books, &c. &c., and a window crowded with piscatorial attractions, of which not the least attractive is a six-pound trout, I turn the handle and enter. Before me extends an immense room, about a hundred feet long, the upper portion enclosed for an office, while the long walls on either side are stored with every machination the fertile brain of man ever invented to entrap the unwary inhabitants of the liquid element.

As I turn to the left, and lean upon an immense show-case, standing detached and filled with attractive lures, I find myself at the elbow of Michael, one of the *attachés* of the premises. Here I must come to a halt for a moment. I cannot without a good word pass an old friend, and he one of the most expert fishermen and most perfect fly-tiers I ever met. And more than that, Michael comes from a neighbourhood I know well. Until a year or two since, he lived near Fermoy, and was a constant attendant on the officers of that garrison. There is not a hole, a stream, a stretch of dead-water within ten miles of that town, whether it be on the Blackwater, Bride, Phuncheon or Araglen, that he is not acquainted with. Before him, as he sits, are ranged gut, hackles, golden and European pheasant feathers, hooks, silk, and wax, for day after day, unless he takes a holiday, his deft fingers are tying salmon or trout flies. As soon as Michael sees me, he clears a seat, and, at his request, I sit down and go to work, just, as he says, to keep my hand in. Of course the old country, and the neighbourhood of Fermoy, and the gentry, are the staple of conversation, with an occasional inquiry after old military acquaintances, whose cicerone he was wont to be.

When abroad, how pleasant it is to talk of home! how the warm blood of affection rushes to your heart when the thoughts wander back to the land of your nativity! But Doctor Clerk has seen me enter, and here he comes with a good-natured smile on his face, which I know predicts an invitation to lunch; if I had eaten ten previously that day I will accept it; for from the Doctor I shall learn more of salmon fishing, as well as of the habits and peculiarities of Mr. Salmo Salar, than from any one I ever met. The Doctor, who is quite a naturalist, has killed salmon from his own native Scotch stream to the rivers that enter the Pacific; of late years he has wandered less, still no season passes without his finding his way to Nova Scotia, New Brunswick, or Labrador. Report says that he can beat all comers at throwing a long and light line. I know that few, very few, can tie such a perfect salmon-fly. After the Doctor and self have greeted one another, we pass on, taking a casual look at what appears most attractive. American reels, of which there appears an immense stock, excite much my admiration, they are all so superiorly finished. One that I am shown, but is not for sale, and is the first ever made, is constructed out of pure aluminium; the mechanism is perfect, the weight is a mere trifle, and there is no amount of exposure will cause it to corrode.

The Yankees are wondrous smart fellows; their wits

appear never to be at rest, and the number of artificial baits that have emanated from their brains is truly surprising. Buell-spoons, kill-jacks, phantom-minnows, and, and—but their name is legion, and certainly many are very deadly.

Boxes of gut, feathers, hooks, lines, rods, lie ranged around; the farther up the store you advance the more you see, till the brain becomes mystified, in wondering what portion of the earth did not assist in supplying a portion of the collection. Through the credit of Messrs. Brown Brothers and Co., of New York and London, the Clerks import direct the well-known bamboo of Calcutta, and the more tough and tapering bamboos of Japan. India and Japan furnish their silk lines, and the tropical climes of both continents are ransacked to supply them with feathers.

An hour has already flitted past, still not one-tenth of the curios have been seen,—but here comes the junior partner; his eye is sharp and keen; you may bet that he can strike quick and certain when a trout rises at his fly. It is so; and not a brook near New York has not over and over again yielded her brilliant beauties to fill his basket.

On reaching the office at the top of the store we find the head of the firm, who is not one particle less genial than his *confrères*. From him I learn that the split bamboo fly-rods are finished, and one of the clerks is ordered to produce them for inspection. Gently, handle them gently, for never did fair woman merit kind treatment more than these treasures at the hand of one who knows their use and value. Each one is put together, each joint fits as close as the cylinder of a steam-engine, and turn them as you will no warp or cast can be seen; twelve feet long is each, not over six ounces in weight, and a four-pound trout, if drawn out by the hair of his head, would not break them.

Their balance on examination proves perfect, and the only regret that creeps over me is, that I have not a cast of flies on, and am situated by the margin of a well-stocked stream. Yes! they are worthy of the friends for whom they are intended, and more than worthy of all I have said in their praise. But to lunch No. 2 I must go; the Doctor is impatient, and I wish to learn a new wrinkle in taking salmon. Before I get out of the door, however, I am asked if I would not like to see another floor. "Another floor!" I internally ejaculated; "no, I thank you,"—*sotto voce*. By Jemminy, if I did, I should dream of fish and fishing, hooks, feathers and gut, every night for the rest of the week. If any of my readers chance to be in New York, rain or sunshine, frost or thaw, if they be disciples of old Izaak Walton, if they want information on affairs piscatorial, whether they require tackle or not, let them visit the hospitable firm of Messrs. Clerk & Co., Maiden Lane, for well am I aware that they will never think the time thus spent thrown away.

THE END.

M. FIGUIER'S BOOKS.

―o―

Sixth Thousand, in One Volume, Demy 8vo., cloth extra, price 16s.

THE WORLD BEFORE THE DELUGE.

With 25 Ideal Landscapes of the Ancient World, designed by Riou, and 208 Figures of Animals, Plants, and other Fossil Remains and Restorations. Third Edition. The Geological portion carefully revised, and much original matter added by H. W. BRISTOW, F.R S., of the Geological Survey of Great Britain.

Fourth Thousand, in One Volume, Demy 8vo., cloth extra, price 16s.

THE VEGETABLE WORLD:

BEING A HISTORY OF PLANTS, WITH THEIR BOTANICAL DESCRIPTION AND PECULIAR PROPERTIES.

With 470 Engravings, chiefly drawn from nature by M. Faquet.

Fourth Thousand, in One Volume, Demy 8vo., cloth extra, price 16s.

THE INSECT WORLD.

New Edition, revised and corrected by E. W. JANSON, Librn. E.S. With 576 Illustrations.

Fourth Thousand, in One Volume, Demy 8vo., cloth extra, price 16s.

THE OCEAN WORLD.

With 427 Illustrations.

CHAPMAN AND HALL, 193, PICCADILLY.

CHAPMAN & HALL'S SERIES OF POPULAR AND STANDARD BOOKS.

Strongly bound in Cloth. 5s. each.

BONES AND I; or, The Skeleton at Home. By J. G. Whyte-Melville. Crown 8vo. 5s.

CERISE; a Tale of the Last Century. By J. G. Whyte-Melville. Fourth Edition. Crown 8vo. 5s. With a Frontispiece.

THE BROOKE OF BRIDLEMERE. By J. G. Whyte-Melville. Crown 8vo. 5s. With a Frontispiece.

THE WHITE ROSE. By J. G. Whyte-Melville. Crown 8vo. 5s.

UNDER TWO FLAGS. A Novel. By "Ouida." Crown 8vo. 5s.

CHANDOS. A Novel. By "Ouida." Crown 8vo. 5s.

STRATHMORE. A Novel. By "Ouida." Crown 8vo. 5s.

IDALIA. A Novel. By "Ouida." Crown 8vo. 5s.

CECIL CASTLEMAINE'S GAGE, and other Novelettes. By "Ouida." Crown 8vo. 5s.

THE SHAVING OF SHAGPAT. By George Meredith. Crown 8vo., with a Frontispiece. 5s.

THE AUTHOR OF "FLEMISH INTERIORS."

FEUDAL CASTLES OF FRANCE (Western Provinces). By the Author of "Flemish Interiors," &c., &c. Illustrated from the Author's Sketches. Demy 8vo. 14s.

GHEEL; the City of the Simple. By the Author of "Flemish Interiors." Crown 8vo. 6s.

E. B. EASTWICK, C.B., F.R.S., &c.

VENEZUELA: or, Sketches of Life in a South American Republic; with the History of the Loan of 1864. By Edward B. Eastwick, C.B., F.R.S., late Secretary of Legation at the Court of Persia, &c. Demy 8vo., with Map. 16s.

ISABELLE SAXON.

FIVE YEARS WITHIN THE GOLDEN GATE (San Francisco). By Isabelle Saxon. Post 8vo. 9s.

W. HEPWORTH DIXON.

THE HOLY LAND. By William Hepworth Dixon. With Illustrations from Original Drawings and Photographs. Fourth edition. Crown 8vo. 10s. 6d.

HOWARD HOPLEY.

UNDER EGYPTIAN PALMS; or, Three Bachelors' Journeyings on the Nile. By Howard Hopley. Crown 8vo. 8s.

DR. PAIJKULL.

A SUMMER IN ICELAND. By C. W. Paijkull, Professor of Geology at the University of Upsala. Translated by the Rev. M. R. Barnard, B.A. Illustrated. Demy 8vo. 14s.

A TRAVELLING ATLAS OF THE ENGLISH COUNTIES. By Sidney Hall. Fifty Coloured Maps. New Edition, with Railways to present time. Demy 8vo., roan tuck. 10s. 6d.

CHAPMAN AND HALL, 193, PICCADILLY.

GEORGE ROOPER.

FLOOD, FIELD, AND FOREST. By George Rooper. With Illustrations. Post 8vo. 8s.

"The story of 'Bolsover Forest' has a strong human interest . . . well constructed, energetically carried out, and essentially dramatic in its character. . . . We feel a personal obligation to Mr. Rooper for the pleasure his writings have afforded us."—*Land and Water.*

"The whole life of the fox . . . is told with great spirit and interest."—*Spectator.*

UBIQUE.

GUN, ROD, AND SADDLE. Personal Experiences. By Ubique. Crown 8vo. 7s. 6d.

"The general public will fully enjoy these reminiscences of sport and adventure, which are told in a frank, straightforward way, without any attempt at effect, or any romantic embellishments."—*Athenæum.*

"Contains many valuable hints and suggestions, based on long practical experience, of which younger and more untried sportsmen may do well to avail themselves."—*Morning Post.*

"'Ubique's' book is well worth reading, and there is an air of candour about it, that convinces us his most wonderful traveller's tales are facts not fictions."—*Pall Mall Gazette.*

R. ARTHUR ARNOLD.

FROM THE LEVANT, THE BLACK SEA, AND THE DANUBE. By R. Arthur Arnold, Author of "The History of the Cotton Famine," &c., &c. 2 vols., post 8vo. 20s.

"As a *dilettante* traveller we have nothing but praise for Mr. Arnold. He has an artist's eye, and the gift of making his reader share his admiration. He succeeds in reproducing lights and shadows as well as outline. . . . Mr. Arnold's descriptions are as lucid and as little dull as may be, and he brings far more classical lore to the hunting up the old classical memories than the average cultivated Englishman would carry with him. . . . We are sure he is always frank and honest: and what we want in 'Letters from the Levant' is truth even more than wisdom."—*Times.*

C. O. GROOM NAPIER.

TOMMY TRY, and what he did in Science. By Charles Otley Groom Napier (of Merchiston), F.G.S., &c. With 46 Illustrations engraved by J. D. Cooper and others. Crown 8vo. 6s.

"A good and pleasant little book is 'Tommy Try.' Besides conveying to youth information on subjects that invariably interest them, it is written in an airy spirit, well calculated to entice their attention."—*Daily Telegraph.*

A. STEINMETZ.

THE ROMANCE OF DUELLING IN ALL TIMES AND COUNTRIES. By Andrew Steinmetz, Author of "The History of the Jesuits," &c. 2 vols., post 8vo. 21s.

WALTER WHITE.

A MONTH IN YORKSHIRE. By Walter White. Fourth Edition, with a Map. Crown 8vo. 4s.

A LONDONER'S WALK TO THE LAND'S END, and a Trip to the Scilly Isles. By Walter White. Second Edition, with 4 Maps. Crown 8vo. 4s.

CHAPMAN AND HALL, 193, PICCADILLY.

Nearly ready, in Two handsome Volumes, with Illustrations and Maps, Demy 8vo.

NEW TRACKS IN NORTH AMERICA:

Being a Narrative of Explorations, Travels, and Adventures in the South-Western Territories of the United States. Containing an Account of the Aztec Inhabitants, and the Results of the Recent Survey for a Southern Railway to the Pacific Ocean.

By Dr. W. A. BELL, F.R.G.S.

DOTTINGS ON THE ROADSIDE,

IN THE

ISTHMUS OF PANAMA, CENTRAL AMERICA, AND THE MOSQUITO COUNTRY.

By COMMANDER BEDFORD PIM, R.N., F.R.G.S., &c., AND DR. BERTHOLD SEEMANN, F.L.S., F.R.G.S.

Illustrated with Plates and Maps. 18s.

FOREST LIFE IN ACADIE.

Sketches of Sport and Natural History in the Lower Provinces of the Canadian Frontier.

By CAPTAIN CAMPBELL HARDY, R.A.

With Coloured Frontispiece and Illustrations. Demy. 18s.

In One handsome Volume, Imperial 8vo., price 42s.

UNDERGROUND LIFE;

OR, MINES AND MINERS.

By L. SIMONIN.

Translated, adapted to the present state of British Mining, and edited by H. W. BRISTOW, F.R.S., of the Geological Survey; Hon. Fellow of King's College, London. Illustrated with 160 Engravings on Wood, 20 Maps Geologically Coloured, and 10 Plates of Metals and Minerals in Chromo-lithography.

In One handsome Volume, Demy 8vo., price 18s.

OUR LIFE IN JAPAN.

By R. MOUNTENEY JEPHSON AND E. PENNELL ELMHIRST, 9th Regiment.

With 20 Illustrations from Photographs by Lord Walter Kerr, Signor Beato, and from native Japanese Drawings.

CHAPMAN AND HALL, 193, PICCADILLY.